TEN OF HEARTS

The Heart of Midlothian Story 1980 – 1990

RAY HEPBURN

INTRODUCTION BY **WALLACE MERCER**

MAINSTREAM
PUBLISHING

First published in great Britain 1990 by
MAINSTREAM PUBLISHING COMPANY (EDINBURGH) LTD
7 Albany Street
Edinburgh EH1 3UG

British Library Cataloguing in Publication Data
Hepburn, Ray
    Ten of Hearts : a decade at Tynecastle
    1. Scotland. Association football. Clubs: Heart of
    Midlothian Football Club, history
    I. Title
    796.33463094134

    ISBN 1-85158-392-0

Typeset in Plantin Expanded by
IPEK Origination Ltd, Edinburgh
Printed in Great Britain by
Billings & Sons, Worcester

This book is dedicated to the memory of John Fairgrieve
Dear friend and much missed colleague.

Contents

INTRODUCTION
by A. Wallace Mercer
Chairman, Heart of Midlothian
Football Club

THE DECADE that my colleagues and I have been through at Tynecastle has surely been among the most tumultuous ever experienced by any football club in this country. From the drastic financial position of the club when I took over in May 1981, through managerial changes and a dramatic turnover in playing staff, the developments that have turned the club into the third top in Scotland have at times been breathtaking. But it is with a degree of satisfaction that we can look back on our efforts, whilst still possessing the ambition to take the whole exercise that one step further and bring a trophy to Tynecastle for our supporters.

The board have moved to meet that challenge with the appointment of Joe Jordan as our manager and, in looking forward with optimism with the team under his leadership, this is also an opportunity to reflect on what has gone before.

I would like to place on record the board's appreciation for the work and achievements that Alex MacDonald and Sandy Jardine, and their back-room staff, have fashioned over the years. The decisions to make changes over the years were not easy. They never are, but when we acted, it was because we felt it necessary.

Looking back, there have been disappointments, but happily they have been outnumbered by many marvellous evenings of high drama, both here and further afield. Our experience in European competition, which seemed a million miles away at the start of the Eighties, has been memorable.

In playing terms, then, we have progressed from the Scottish First Division into being regular competitors on the European stage, and financially, from making deals that sometimes involved hundreds of pounds, we can now scan the transfer market at the very highest level. For all these reasons, the board thought it appropriate to record in book form the ten years that made the

Eighties so exciting. In words and pictures, this volume collates the good times and the bad.

The author has chosen to record each chapter around one member of the staff at Hearts whom he considers to have been particularly influential through the club's development. It is, then, the official club record of a period that I personally would not have missed for the world.

The ten years represented in these pages have made this great club what it is now. The board of Heart of Midlothian Football Club are proud of them. I, as Chairman, am sure you are too and hope that whilst reading *Ten of Hearts* we can all draw inspiration from the club's history and together go on to bigger and better things.

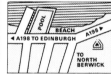

CHAPTER ONE

Alex MacDonald
1980-81

THE NEWS that Alex MacDonald had been sacked as manager of Hearts, along with his assistant, Walter Borthwick, sent shock waves through Scottish football just two days before John Robertson was to make his début for Scotland in the 2-1 victory over Romania in the European Championships. At Tynecastle, though, there had been a feeling in the early weeks of the 1990-91 season that all was not well. Players felt that there was a new tension in the air around the club, and there was no doubt that three successive defeats by Premier Division teams placed extra pressure on everyone.

After St Mirren had been defeated in a Skol Cup replay at Love Street, the sequence that was to have such a dramatic effect on the club started with a 2-0 defeat at Dunfermline, a ground where Hearts had performed so well in the previous season.

Then it was on to Aberdeen, where a performance and result similar to the one that had ended Scottish Cup hopes the previous season was repeated as Alex Smith's players continued to give the impression that they were the in-form team in the early part of the campaign.

That was in the Skol Cup, and after that match a small section of the travelling Hearts support, depleted by the live BSB showing of the match, called for MacDonald to be replaced. This small demonstration weighed heavily on Chairman Wallace Mercer's mind during the seemingly endless journey back from the north, for he revealed later that he was determined the calls from the terraces should not be allowed to increase in volume and make it impossible for the manager to stay.

Four days later, Rangers travelled to Tynecastle and, although George Wright pulled Hearts back into the game with three minutes remaining, after Peter Huistra and Ally McCoist had placed Rangers in a winning position, salvation was elusive and McCoist immediately re-established Rangers' two-goal advantage.

Less than an hour after Hearts' second home Premier Division match of the season, the board were meeting at Tynecastle and the decision that a change must be made was taken. Alex and Walter were informed of the board's decision on the Monday morning, and, just five days ahead of the first derby of the season, the reverberations of the news sent one half of Edinburgh into deep shock.

At the press conference three hours after the original announcement, Mercer was to explain that, before taking such a major step, he too had offered to stand down from chairmanship, but having accepted the support of the board, their decision was unanimous.

Both men left Tynecastle quickly, but not before MacDonald had, typically, despite the high emotion that overtook more than him on that day, walked round every member of the staff at Hearts to shake their hands, thank them and wish them well for the future.

After ten years there were many red eyes scattered around the place as the board faced the task of starting the selection process for a successor, but just as importantly, and more timely, setting in motion a short-term regime that would carry Hearts into a crucial period. Sandy Clark, who had returned to the club to a coaching position after a brief, unhappy spell as manager of Partick Thistle, took charge of first team matters but John Binnie, who would have been made responsible for the reserve side, resigned after 24 hours' consideration. Clark was able to call on the assistance of the senior players at Tynecastle, and within a couple of days David McCreery had taken the third team to Tannadice for a match against Dundee United.

Typically, as he gathered his thoughts just hours after hearing the news, MacDonald was to think of the players and supporters he had grown so close to during the Eighties in his first public response. He said, 'After hitting the post so often during the last few years, it would have been nice to have left the club having given the players and supporters a trophy to enjoy from my spell in charge.'

Wallace Mercer then went on to explain that the club were looking for a new man to take them into a new era, but not before he had paid glowing tribute to the man he had grown up with, and

Looking ahead – Alex MacDonald and Wallace Mercer

learned with, during his early football days. He explained, 'Together, Alex MacDonald and I helped save this club from extinction and his contribution to that effort can never be questioned. But the signs had been there in recent matches, and we simply could not ignore that. The whole dynamics of football in Scotland have changed, we must move with the times, and felt to accommodate the new circumstances a new management structure was inevitable.'

But it is still fitting that the chronicle of the Eighties should start with Alex MacDonald. Not only because Bobby Moncur brought him to Tynecastle from Rangers on 8 August, 1980, and therefore his career with Hearts fits neatly into the time span we are dealing with.

Much more importantly, MacDonald's presence and influence as a player, captain and manager have without doubt been a most significant factor in a period that has established the club once again as one of Scotland's greatest.

Off the field, as we will discover later, the dynamic Wallace Mercer appeared one year later to steer things in the right direction indoors. This unlikely duo came together at the right time, in the right place, and Hearts were the benefactors.

MacDonald, 32 by the time he brought his wealth of experience to the Capital, had established himself as one of the most respected of Scotland's professionals for almost two decades. Despite having played more football than most in his generation, all his thoughts were geared towards continuing simply as a player. He had given no thought to football management. Not that that was a factor at the time, for in Bobby Moncur the club was being led by a man who, in hindsight, placed a correct emphasis on recruiting young players from the Edinburgh area, and who possessed a tremendous reputation as a player both at club level with Newcastle and in the international arena.

However, the task that faced Hearts that season was a formidable one. The Premier Division at that time was at its most competitive, with Rangers and Celtic making their predictable push for prizes, but the whole conundrum had been complicated with the emergence of the 'New Firm'. Dundee United had finally shed their image as a nearly club by winning the League Cup, and Aberdeen, also recent winners of that competition and in the previous season the Premier Division, were on the point of developing the winning habit to the stage of near-excellence.

But if age seemed against MacDonald as he sought to use his influence as a catalyst for stability with a team which had travelled into the decade as Division One champions, having won that title by two points from Airdrie, with Ayr United a further seven points adrift in third place, there was no doubting the value of his experience. A proud Glaswegian, MacDonald's first taste of competitive team football came at the age of nine with the local Life Boys' team. Jimmy Lumsden's father ran the team and that was to be the start of a friendship which exists to this day. Indeed, the former Celtic player has been MacDonald's eyes and ears in the lower divisions in England for many seasons. Therefore, when players like Mike Galloway, Neil Berry, Wayne Foster and Mark Gavin were arriving at Tynecastle with virtually no financial outlay toward the end of this decade, Lumsden's opinion was sought in every instance.

The Crookston Street School side was MacDonald's next development stage, and although his height at that age was always a disadvantage, as is always the case in youth football, he quickly discovered and developed qualities of a battler that are still a vital element of his character to this day.

At 14, he moved into the Under-18 juvenile ranks with a quaintly named team called Plantation Hearts. The obvious pun that this might have been an earlier nursery for the Edinburgh variety should be avoided. In 1966 it was good that his move into junior football should be with Glasgow United, for they had a long established record of providing players for the senior game and, with that reputation intact, their matches were constantly watched by senior scouts.

It took no time at all for St Johnstone to be convinced that MacDonald had all the qualities they required. The then manager, Bobby Brown, a former Scotland team boss, was certain that he would have to move quickly for a young man who had created a big impression as a striker. Recalled Brown, 'In his second trial match for us he scored two goals against Dundee United and I knew at the time that there were more people than me on his trail. I tried to fix him up there and then. But he, although seeming quite keen, didn't want to commit himself until he'd had the chance to discuss the situation with his grandmother. To this day I don't know what she told him, but it did the trick and soon after he became a St Johnstone player.

'The speed with which we moved turned out to be crucial, for I later learned that Newcastle United were on the way north to offer him terms as well, and there is no doubt in my mind that he was one of my best ever signings.'

Brown was struck immediately with the confidence that his new acquisition possessed. Not cockiness, but a control and comfort in his surroundings that left him completely devoid of any temptation to feel overawed in his new circumstances. He was also to spot an attribute that would assist MacDonald to become one of Scotland's most respected club managers: an ability to read developments in a game quickly, and assess the intentions of older players in opposition.

On his way to training at Muirton every day MacDonald passed Ibrox and when in 1968 Rangers paid the then considerable £50,000 transfer fee for a player who had by now found his niche as a wing half, a lifetime's ambition was complete.

'I basically didn't show any form at all in my first year with Rangers. I spent most of the time pinching myself to make sure what was happening was true,' he remembers.

It was at that time he developed the deep friendship he still enjoys with Sandy Jardine. They roomed together whenever Rangers were abroad, played together for two decades at Rangers and Hearts, and of course were a highly successful management team for most of the Eighties at Tynecastle.

'Sandy to this day is still someone whose opinion I listen to. When we were players together it always struck me as being particularly generous, the way he would share information with me, and we built up a mutual respect that will last a lifetime,' he added.

The prizes with the great Seventies Rangers team rolled in. He's the proud winner of three League Championship medals, four Scottish Cup and League Cup badges, one Glasgow Cup medal and his prize possession. The reminder of the night in Barcelona when Rangers defeated Moscow Dynamo 3-2 on 24 May, 1972. Jardine, Alfie Conn and Willie Johnston, who were all to contribute to the Hearts effort during the Eighties, were in that side as well. So too was Peter McCloy who, in his capacity as a freelance coach, is regarded by current 'keeper, Henry Smith, as a crucial influence in his game and his in ability to sustain form in the coming years at the highest level.

During that playing time at Ibrox there was also the thrill, and the great pride, of turning out for the 'one and only time' with Scotland. That was in 1976 when Willie Ormond was in charge. The opponents were Switzerland at Hampden in May of that year.

16

Willie Pettigrew, another player who was to travel the Tynecastle road later, made a scoring début that night in a 1-0 victory. Alan Rough, who was to go on to win 53 caps over more than a decade as Scotland's number one, also made his début in that match.

It is not surprising then, that with his ability to absorb information and the subsequent realisation that he could, with authority, pass it on he should develop into such an accomplished manager. However, his transition from the dressing-room to the gaffer's office owes much to aspects of human make-up that are prerequisites of success in any walk of life.

The confidence of which Bobby Brown had been an earlier witness makes him an outstanding motivator. The time for a manager to move on is when the players do not listen with instant belief to what is being said. At Hearts, when MacDonald spoke there was no whispering in corners or giggling behind his back.

He is, too, an honest man – which in professional football these days is increasingly rare. In the day to day contact between football manager and journalists there are bound to be circumstances when different interests clash. It is inevitable that there will be information which the journalist seeks that the football man is unwilling to communicate. To do so may well jeopardise a transfer at a delicate stage, or perhaps alert opponents to a weakness in the case of injury or suspension. Little white lies are therefore allowed and accepted. But lies do not slip comfortably off MacDonald's tongue. Where many of his contemporaries are happy to lie their way out of an awkward question, he will simply choose to avoid an answer...allowing the questioner to make his mind up for himself.

It has also been possible for me to observe a tremendous loyalty factor in his make-up. There are those who would argue that in team selection matters, that can be a negative. That may well be the case, but the positives attached to such an attribute will always make loyalty something to envy. His impact in the dressing-room at Tynecastle gave credence to that argument.

I can recall travelling with Hearts to Czechoslovakia for their UEFA Cup-tie against Dukla Prague in 1986 where I was able to witness all these characteristics first hand.

At that time I had a good working relationship with Mac-Donald, although it would be fair to say that we did not know each other all that well and there was no need for him to consider that I should be the recipient of any special favours.

On the morning of the match, in the Intercontinental Hotel in Prague, I received a telephone call from Geoffrey Webster, who was at that time, and is once again, Head of BBC Radio Sport in Glasgow, asking if I could cover the Second Leg tie. The match was being played in the late afternoon and with the time difference Hearts' fate that season would be known before the BBC's main sports programme started at 7.30 p.m. In addition to filing a match report by telephone from the hotel after the game, Webster asked if I could arrange an interview with MacDonald.

Bearing in mind that football managers, quite understandably, sometimes find it difficult to fulfil radio work in the midst of deep disappointment should things go wrong on the day, I warned that, dependent on the result, the interview might or might not be possible. Before the game, then, I asked Alex if he would talk through me to the BBC once we got back to the hotel. He asked, 'Do I have to tell you now?' I replied that, of course, no, there was no need to commit himself at that time and that he and the players, I understood, had a much more pressing priority earlier in the day to see to, and we would see how things were at the end of the match.

In the event, a single Griga goal in far-off Prague meant that Hearts would go out on goal difference and, while the team changed in the spartan dressing-room in Dukla's massive stadium next to the Army barracks which betrayed the club's roots, I sped off in a taxi to the hotel.

I had just completed a match report for the *Glasgow Herald* when it was time for the BBC to call, and when I was connected by the producer to the programme output, I could hear Tom Ferrie preparing to come live to me in Prague in around 40 seconds. Suddenly there was a knock at the door. Not knowing whether to hold on for that brief time for the interview, or answer it, I threw the phone down and dashed to the door to find the Hearts manager waiting at the other side. The deep disappointment at the outcome of the match was still written all over his nervous face when he asked, 'Do you still want me to do this interview?'

We raced over to the phone to pick it up five seconds before Ferrie was to introduce the report. Although during the course of the next couple of minutes Alex MacDonald and I disagreed over a goal that Hearts had had disallowed for offside, he completed the

18

interview with his usual competence and even a little humour. That, for me, is Alex MacDonald.

Jardine, MacDonald has acknowledged, has been a great influence in his career, but so too, he will tell you, have Willie Waddell and Jock Wallace, and perhaps the former Hearts coach and Rangers manager has been the greatest of them all.

Wallace was coach at Rangers when MacDonald moved from St Johnstone, and it was from him that he learned the value for any professional athlete of fastidiously looking after the body. MacDonald tends his with the care that a sculptor protects his chisels, and a musician his instruments. And it was from the early days at Ibrox that MacDonald learned of the benefits of annual slogs up and down the sand dunes at Gullane. 'It's quite simple. If you don't get the engine right from the start, you're going to get mechanical problems all the way through. There is no chance of a footballer catching up during the course of a season what he has failed to do in the preparation fitness work. However, the opposite also applies. If the groundwork has been done in advance, all that is required when the games start is a topping up exercise,' insists MacDonald.

It's ironic that Wallace, who was such a fitness fanatic in his time, should now find himself inhibited by Parkinson's Disease, for which he's now a tireless worker. His regard for MacDonald is firm and sure.

'From the very first time I saw Alex I knew we were dealing with a very special player and, although he took a little time to settle at Ibrox, one thing that struck me early on was his tremendous stamina,' reflected Wallace. 'There is no doubt that the tremendous respect with which he's looked after himself through the years enabled him to play at Premier League and European level well into the Eighties. Coupled with his willingness to learn, the combination was always going to ensure that Alex would make an outstanding manager.'

However, it was, to repeat, as a player that Hearts would first make demands on him. But in that first season the task that lay ahead presented a formidable challenge.

There was an early taste of things to come when five matches prior to the start of the Premier Division programme yielded not one victory. There were defeats by Chelsea and Airdrie, and draws against Glenavon in Ireland and with Newcastle and Airdrie at

Robertson senior – Chris on target at Montrose

home. The one bright spot as the team prepared for an away fixture at Firhill was the way Chris Robertson and Derek O'Connor were finding the net. Chris had three goals to his credit by the opening day and Derek two.

At this time, the younger version of the Robertson family, John, was only 16 but was already looking a tremendous prospect in the reserves and, as the season proper approached, Chris was to say prophetically, 'If he continues to work hard enough, he's certain to have a successful career... I'll have to watch out for my place.'

Despite MacDonald making his début, and with new signings Robertson, Alfie Conn and Willie McVie coming in against Partick Thistle, there was no respite in Glasgow. Thistle were 3-2 winners with Frank Liddell and Cammy Fraser scoring Hearts' goals from the penalty spot.

Then followed two fixtures without a goal, both at Tynecastle – a 0-0 draw against Berwick in the East of Scotland Shield and then a 2-0 defeat by Airdrie – as the team still searched for their first league points of the season.

18 YEARS
AT THE
TOP OF
THEIR LEAGUE

AND NEVER IN DANGER
OF RELEGATION!

Spot the Hearts connection! Derek O'Connor, Sandy Jardine and Peter McCloy

Two Willie Gibson goals halted that brief trend in an East of Scotland Shield match against Hibs at home, which was to be the forerunner of that long awaited first League victory. O'Connor was again the main hitman, with two goals, and Alfie Conn scored a third in an impressive 3-1 victory.

Things brightened up, and, although in the first week of September, a Chris Robertson goal and a David Bowman strike were not sufficient to avoid a 3-2 defeat by Ayr at home in the League Cup, there had been two earlier victories against Montrose in the same competition. Again Robertson led the way in the home match with the opening goal, followed by MacDonald's début goal for Hearts... the result 2-1. Even better was to follow at tiny Links Park when Robertson grabbed a hat-trick as Hearts travelled back south 3-1 victors before, later in the month, a 4-0 drubbing at Ayr in the second leg of the tie was to end the club's interests in the League Cup.

Premier League points were always going to be the main

Doddy jumps to it – against Airdrie

priority and things looked bright down at Rugby Park on 6 September when Willie Gibson scored the only goal of the match against Kilmarnock to record a second successive away win in the championship . . . but gloom was quickly to follow. Home defeats by Celtic, 2-0, and Ayr United, by a single goal to nil, sent the players to Tannadice where Derek O'Connor was the scorer in a 1-1 draw.

Then followed eight successive Premier Division matches without a victory that would ultimately make the task of staying in the top ten beyond the team. Aberdeen, Rangers, Partick Thistle, Airdrie and Dundee United were all winners against Hearts, while there were draws with St Mirren, Morton and the Ibrox team. In that dismal spell containing 12 hours of football, Alfie Conn scored twice, MacDonald once and O'Connor once, before another victory was finally achieved.

MacDonald and Paul O'Brien grabbed home goals against Kilmarnock but the two points offered only brief respite for, despite goals by MacDonald and Gibson at Celtic Park a week

Derek O'Connor – the heap man against East Fife

later, the team went down 3-2, setting off in the third week of December another disastrous sequence which would last until March. Heading for Christmas, there was a dour 0-0 draw with Morton at Tynecastle and then the day after Boxing Day, a 4-1 defeat by Dundee United on Tayside, when Willie Gibson was the consolation goal-getter. He did the trick again on New Year's Day, as did Paul O'Brien, but they were not enough to fend off a 3-2 home defeat by Airdrie to deflate the Hogmanay celebrations, and those who travelled to Firhill on 3 January were hardly cheered by the 1-0 Partick win.

MacDonald had during this period been standing skipper after a suspension halted Jim Jefferies' first-team run, and when the rugged defender was able to return following his ban, manager Bobby Moncur decided that Alex would continue in a position he clearly relished. Already, his dedicated professional approach to the game had commanded the respect of the Hearts squad at the time which was, in a full-time way, soon to lose Derek O'Connor. Persistent knee trouble resulted in medical advice that involved turning to part-time football and a less strenuous physical regime as a remedy.

But still the results wouldn't turn and, after losing 2-0 at home against Aberdeen, Hearts were to go out of the Scottish Cup at the hands of Morton. There were no goals in the first match at Tynecastle but in the replay, at Cappielow, despite a tremendous following from Edinburgh in a crowd of almost 10,000 fans, Alex MacDonald's goal could not avert a 3-1 exit from the national association's knockout tournament. The league position had become desperate and certainly wasn't helped by a 3-0 defeat at the hands of Celtic and then a 2-1 reverse at Love Street when Pat McShane was the club's scorer. MacDonald and the experienced Peter Shields were both absent that day and McShane's first Premier Division goal came during a second half in which the team's performance probably merited a point. On the plus side, Gary Liddell made his début and Jim Jefferies was recovering from a training injury that followed his lengthy suspension.

A Walter Kidd goal and a home draw against Partick Thistle was the prelude to another heavy defeat around the corner at Pittodrie, when Alex Hamill was the Hearts scorer in a 4-1 defeat.

However, on 14 March there was some consolation at Tynecastle in the 2-1 defeat of Rangers, when an own goal and a Frank Liddell effort produced some encouragement for the future . . . although it hardly seemed that way in the following four weeks. Kilmarnock and Hearts had become so divorced from the pack that pride was all that was left in the remaining matches. There was precious little of that to take from four successive defeats. Morton, Kilmarnock, Dundee United and Celtic were all successive winners against Hearts and they scored 15 goals with not a single, solitary reply in the process to send the team lurching toward Division One in even more despondency.

David Bowman who, like Gary Mackay, was being forced to carry too much responsibility at the age of only 17, scored the winning goal against Kilmarnock at Rugby Park in the first week of April, and then successive defeats by Aberdeen and St Mirren, where young Scott Maxwell was on target, were to precede the final victory of the season. Gary Liddell's first goals for Hearts won the day against Airdrie at Broomfield before MacDonald's first season at Tynecastle was to end, ironically, at Ibrox with

Rangers' 4-0 victory to complete a miserable Premier Division season.

At least, however, on and off the pitch things had become so bad that only drastic action would fashion the right kind of change. The boardroom turmoil that would follow in the weeks ahead and the management changes in the course of the next season would set Hearts on the right road.

Even at this stage MacDonald still had no managerial ambitions although in the fullness of time the incoming chairman, Wallace Mercer, was to see in him the qualities that had attracted Jock Wallace so many years before, and his appointment would lead Hearts back into the challenge for honours. Twice, he took his players to within one place of winning the Premier Division Championship and on one occasion to the Scottish Cup final. In a classic image of the football manager's lot, he had manufactured for himself the stick with which he would eventually be beaten.

Even the most cursory study of Hearts' progress through the Eighties under first MacDonald and Jardine, and later MacDonald and Walter Borthwick, reveals the comparative ease with which progress was made in the early years. That is not to diminish the achievements.

However, they knew that taking the team that one crucial step toward a trophy was a much more difficult task. In addition, they had to perfect that one final trick, with expectations raised in the boardroom and on the terracing by the significant progress that had been made.

Nothing is forever, especially in football, and it was inevitable that at some time Alex MacDonald and Hearts would part company. Whether it was at the club's instigation, or indeed the manager's, is of no real importance . . . by the nature of things it would happen anyway. What must be a matter of record is MacDonald's contribution at Tynecastle during the Eighties, and the vast contrasts in the two worlds that the club has inhabited during the decade should be set in perspective.

At the end of his first season, Alfie Conn was to leave for Blackpool on a free transfer and Willie Gibson would move to Partick Thistle for £10,000 at a time when other provincial clubs were dealing in six figure transactions as commonplace.

Now Hearts must see their first million-pound transfer on the

The blackest day - Dens Park, Dundee

not–too–distant horizon and the club at the other end of the development scale is now comfortably running three teams well within the current budget. While ten years ago players were scrambling around trying to find gear to train in, and soon a decision would be made to scrap the reserve side altogether, the current crop of players enjoys all the trappings at the top end of the professional sportsman's scale.

   That has been MacDonald's input at Hearts. Over more than a ten-year period he had given the supporters back their pride. In the late Seventies and early Eighties there was almost a stigma attached to being a Hearts' fan. Now, they can reflect on a connection with a club that is the third best supported in the land, by some of the best behaved followers in the land, who will be housed in the years to come in one of the best stadiums in the country.

   The future will take care of itself but as we continue to recall the 1980s through these pages, time will surely allocate Alex MacDonald the greatest tribute that the club can bestow. He is one of the Hearts' greats.

HEARTS

CLUBCALL

0898 12 11 83

COST 44p / MINUTE

33p CHEAP RATE

CHAPTER TWO

Wallace Mercer
1981-82

IT IS STAGGERING to note that from the team that started the Division One campaign in season 1981/82, there are only two of the existing Tynecastle squad still playing for the club. The side that drew 1-1 at Dunfermline on 21 August, 1981 was: Henry Smith, Brian McNeill, Peter Shields, Pat Byrne, Roddy MacDonald, Stewart MacLaren, David Bowman, Garry McCoy, Gary Liddell, Alex Hamill and Walter Kidd. The substitutes were Frank Liddell and Chris Robertson.

That only two players have survived the ravages of a decade, from that opening line-up, indicates the extent of upheaval that Hearts was undergoing. That turmoil was no more in evidence than during the summer of 1981.

The drama, which was to see Mercer in charge, three managers in the course of a season, and a complete financial overhaul of Hearts, started in May when the then chairman, Archie Martin, attempted a financial rescue. The club's debts were of a magnitude that fresh capital had to be found and found quickly. His first move involved an approach to city bookmaker, Kenny Waugh, who until that day had harboured no thoughts of owning a football club. The first bid in this football poker game was Waugh's cheque for £255,000 and it was to Mercer that former player Donald Ford turned in an effort to produce a rival bid.

The club, even with its enormous potential which was not being realised, hardly looked the bargain of the decade. The team had taken only 18 points when being relegated from the Premier Division, and with gates at an all-time low of just over 120,000, the immediate future was grim.

Mercer was already a modest shareholder in Hearts, and in their attempt to raise fresh capital within a rival bid to Waugh's, he was happy to make a contribution of £30,000 in the hope that others in

The power game! On and off the pitch

the community would produce a similar investment and that Hearts' financial trauma would be over.

Ironically, the Scotland/England match at Wembley that year was the match which triggered off Mercer's love affair with football, and saw him become the influence on Hearts which is now a matter of record. 'A further approach was made to me by Ford, raising the stakes considerably, for they now wanted me to come in as the main man and finance a takeover. Although my business was flourishing in Edinburgh, the kind of cash that the club needed was earmarked for other projects,' recalled Mercer.

To this day Mercer consults his wife, Anne, on virtually every issue and this whole new ball game was no different. Her advice on this occasion was to suggest that there may be something wrong with his mental state if he were to get involved to that degree. But Mercer was to learn that weekend that cold, calculated, financial choices in the business world bear no relation at times to similar decisions in the world of football. Although many people still like to describe football as a business, it is a sport where business acumen and thinking can be a distinct advantage.

However, in the heady atmosphere of a Wembley Saturday, especially on a day when Scotland's Tartan Army were to return home singing the praises of a victory over the Auld Enemy, Mercer's resolve was to crumble. Perhaps it was the moment when John Robertson's low, decisive penalty kick sent 50,000 Scots into ecstasy that persuaded him to take the plunge. Certainly the wonderful atmosphere and excitement had persuaded him that football represented a world within which he could comfortably live.

By the end of the month he had matched the rival offer and, with £85,000 from other members of the consortium which backed his bid, a cheque for £350,000 was on the table.

The war of words which inevitably travelled in tandem with the competition for the Tynecastle club continued until 3 June when a deadline was set for the board to make its final decision. Although there were many troubles and dark days ahead, the bright future, within which the club presently exists, was established that day and the first seeds of the current buoyancy in every aspect of the football club were sown.

Bobby Moncur was the manager and in the previous year had introduced marvellous talents in the shape of Gary Mackay, John Robertson and David Bowman to Tynecastle, but his time at the club was soon to end and he was not the only casualty in the opening months of Mercer's reign. Archie Martin had supported the bid by Kenny Waugh, and it did not take outside genius to realise that the co-existence between the new major shareholder and a boardroom opponent could not happily survive. Within days the club's chairman had resigned and Alex Naylor, a city publican, was to become Hearts' third chairman in a period spanning only 14 months. Martin had earlier replaced Bobby Parker. Like players Smith and Kidd, Parker had survived the decade and is still as firmly in place in the Tynecastle boardroom as he was as captain of the team in his marvellous era as a player in the late Fifties/early Sixties.

While the talk in the Capital had been of shares, deals, offers and takeovers, the players during the course of this period were understandably bemused and concerned.

While all the turmoil was continuing I was in Cannes with the Scotland Youth Team, covering an Eight-Nation Invitation Tournament, and from the playing point of view it was evident then that Hearts had a future. Contained within that Scotland Under-17 side were Mackay, Bowman and Ian Westwater. As a point of information, Kenny Black, then in his Rangers days, together with the likes of Paul McStay, Neale Cooper and Brian Rice, represented his country, and so the Tynecastle youngsters

Tony Ford – but not for long

were mixing with, and living comfortably among, the very best talents of the time.

Mackay confessed in the South of France sunshine, 'Things at the club were simply terrible when we left. We just don't know if we will have jobs to return to when we get back.' For a young man who had been chased by Manchester United and Arsenal among many others, it was clearly a worrying time. In the later pages of this book, Mackay will agree with others that Mercer's intervention was the saving of Hearts.

The next casualty to fall was the manager, Moncur, when it became clear in a matter of weeks that the two men would be unlikely to establish a working relationship. Mercer was ruthless, and although quickly learning the football business, was acutely aware of the merits of a new broom. Moncur resigned within a few days and very quickly accepted the post of manager with Plymouth Argyle and, having secured compensation from his ex-manager, Mercer began the search for a successor.

While the team were starting their League Cup section with five points from the first three fixtures against Airdrie, Aberdeen and Kilmarnock, Moncur's assistant, Tony Ford, was left in charge of the first team. While he coped, rather awkwardly, with that responsibility, Mercer set about reconstructing the team with the same clinical relish that had seen the boardroom and the manager's office dramatically altered.

Perhaps in hindsight, not surprisingly, Mercer's eyes drifted upwards in the search for a successor to the former Scotland defender, Moncur. Jock Wallace and Jim McLean, two of the most successful individuals in their profession, were his first choices. While talks with Dundee United over McLean were to elongate and become muddled, the discourse with Wallace, who had been a caretaker manager with Hearts in an earlier time, was typically pointed and brief. 'Y' canny aford me, son, but I'll see you along the road somewhere and all the best for the future,' was his, as always, honest response.

Without an obvious big name that he could trust with the playing side of matters, Mercer decided to give Ford his opportunity, without ever really expecting the arrangement to be a long-term success.

The playing staff was being dramatically trimmed and salaries had already been cut, but with the season taking on a pessimistic appearance, the surgery, it quickly became apparent, might not be sufficient to meet the drastic needs. However, Stewart MacLaren, Derek Strickland, Henry Smith, Roddy MacDonald, Gerry McCoy and Pat Byrne were all recruited, as the reshaping of the team was commenced at a torrid pace. Next, in the autumn, was the purchase, on the never-never, of Willie Pettigrew and Derek Addison, in a deal worth £165,000 which was later to have dramatic consequences for the club.

While all this activity was going on, it was hardly surprising that the team found it difficult to put together any sort of momentum although, in those first three League Cup-ties, single goals from Chris Robertson against Airdrie and Aberdeen had earned victories while Gary Liddell was the marksman in 1-1 Tynecastle draw with Kilmarnock. Three defeats in the second round of section matches ended the team's interest in the tournament and in tandem with that let-down, the first three League games produced only two points. Gary Liddell earned a draw at East End Park and following a 1-0 home defeat by Killie came a no-scoring draw at Brockville.

By mid-September, Pettigrew and Addison were making their débuts, while Gary Mackay was also becoming a regular feature in the starting line-up. Hamilton were beaten 2-1 at Tynecastle with

Willie Pettigrew with scoring space against Clyde

Gary scoring the opener and Alex Hamill adding a second after the break, and then a Derek O'Connor goal safely captured another two points at home against Clydebank.

From there, Somerset Park, Ayr, was the next venue where a 0-0 draw was the reward for travelling west and, after a victory at Dumbarton and a defeat by Queen's Park at Hampden, three straight victories against St Johnstone, Queen of the South and Raith Rovers took the club into mid-October.

Willie Pettigrew scored his first goal for Hearts at Tynecastle against the Perth team, and after that three-win sequence went on to score two more against Motherwell at Fir Park as the hopes for a return to Premier Division football in one season were allowed to rise. That result though was the forerunner of a string of matches that were to see Hearts win just once more in 1981, although in fairness the early cold snap of winter virtually wiped out December and January fixtures. In that spell there were defeats by Dumbarton and East Stirling and draws with Kilmarnock, Dunfermline Athletic and Queen's Park. Addison and Mackay collected the goals at Douglas Park, which were to represent that one crumb of comfort for the winter.

The financing of the transfers which brought Addison and Pettigrew from Tannadice to Tynecastle had depended on selling two players - Peter Shields and Alex MacDonald - and the fact that the two outgoing deals did not materialise presented Mercer with a more calamitous financial position. However, the fact that MacDonald stayed made the temporary financial embarrassment all seem worth the trouble.

The spate of cancellations in December and January and the subsequent lack of income from home matches all added to the pressures on everyone at Tynecastle, and the chairman's patience with Tony Ford had worn thin. It was after the final match against Queen's Park was played, on 5 December, that his position, too, came under stringent review.

The cautious MacDonald, who had been reticent to accept Moncur's offer of the captaincy the previous season, was asked if he would take over team responsibility under the label player/coach . . . and Ford was on his way. Hearts were now being led by two men learning their trade fast.

In the early weeks of 1982 a new set of circumstances dictated that Mercer's introduction to the football boardroom would once again require all his business expertise. Naylor was to be the second Hearts Chairman to resign within months of the new regime being in place. The club had been unable to fulfil its commitment to Dundee United over subsequent payments still due for the Addison-Pettigrew deal, and for the rest of that season Hearts operated without a chairman.

It was around this time that the fledgling football administrator was able to perceive the enormous support and feeling for the club that existed within Edinburgh, and at a time when he might have been excused for cutting and running, Mercer's resolve to succeed at Hearts became more committed.

The club's progress on the playing side resumed at home against Motherwell in the only match that was to go on in January and, despite the fact that the newly recruited Peter Marinello was now in the side, the result was a devastating 3-0 defeat which was to be repeated on the final day of the season as Hearts stayed put in the First Division.

But MacDonald was warming to his new role as player/coach and, after a string of victories that rejuvenated the season in February, he was appointed manager, although no one, including Alex himself, could have believed that he would be there for eight more years, steering the team toward further progress.

That spell, which saw 11 goals scored during an unbeaten four-

Roddy McDonald gets the nod over St Johnstone

game run in the first three weeks of February had East Stirling, Falkirk, Queen of the South and Ayr United as victims. Pettigrew scored three times in the sequence, as did McCoy. Optimism once again took over.

There were away defeats at St Johnstone and Falkirk to follow, however, although the club's capacity to score freely still seemed as if it might be sufficient to earn second place in the table. The Championship was no longer an issue - getting back into the Premier Division was the priority. McCoy scored two more in a 4-0 win over Raith Rovers - Bowman and Chris Robertson scored the others - and then two weeks later the team topped even that, defeating Queen of the South 5-1 at Palmerston. Willie Pettigrew blasted in a hat-trick in that tremendous tonic, and one week later two more precious points were collected at home against Queen's Park, with Pat Byrne the goal-getter, before Kilbowie Park and Clydebank were the March opponents.

The problem in 1982 that was to be so crucial at the end of the season was beginning to form a pattern. If Hearts were not to win a match, although they did so comfortably on many occasions, then they lost. The ability to bite and scratch for a draw on a bad day

Walter whacks it – against St Mirren

was to haunt the team right through to the last day of the season. Clydebank were to mirror that shortcoming and, although Byrne scored from the penalty spot after an hour, the 2-1 defeat saw promotion become less of a reality. But then a dramatic run of victories was to point the team in the direction of a photo-finish.

The run in was by no means easy. The next six weeks pitted Hearts against Raith Rovers, St Johnstone, Hamilton, Clydebank, Ayr United and Dunfermline. Astonishingly, 12 points were taken from six fixtures that represented the most demanding First Division standard and the goals flowed in these games to a degree that everything once again seemed possible. Two each were scored against Hamilton, Ayr and Dunfermline, three were sent past Raith Rovers and St Johnstone, while Clydebank, which had seen disappointment just three weeks earlier, was the venue for a fabulous five-goal treat. At Kilbowie that night Pettigrew scored four times - he was to score 16 in all the Championship that season - while Roddy MacDonald hit the net twice during that run to underline his well-established reputation as an outstanding set-piece raider. Chris Robertson and Gerry McCoy were also among goals with two each.

That left only three matches to be played in the season, against Dumbarton, Kilmarnock and Motherwell . . . the last two against the teams that were eventually to claim the first two places in the league and those coveted spots in the Premier Division.

Sadly, Hearts' vulnerability, as far as having any depth of quality in their squad, was cruelly exposed in the 14 days that featured four and a half hours of football and just one point as reward. Walter Kidd, another Tynecastle favourite, still a valued member of the Hearts staff, and that other vital goal scorer, Roddy MacDonald, missed the last three Saturdays through injury and their absence was to precede a calamitous loss of goals. Byrne and Pettigrew scored in each half at Boghead, but the gaps at the back could not be adequately plugged and the five goals that the Sons scored that Saturday were to leave Hearts level on goal difference going into the away match at Kilmarnock, where Stuart Gauld and Colin More were pulled in at a crucial stage of the campaign.

At Rugby Park changes through injury and suspension seemed to make Kilmarnock odds-on favourites to win the match, but the Ayrshire team, who had already drawn 12 home matches, were unable to overcome Hearts' effort and resilience, and there were no goals scored. There was nothing pretty about the match, and although it was entertaining enough there was precious little fluid football played. More, a part-timer, was playing his first game of the season and, alongside MacLaren in the middle of the back four, performed heroically.

Going in to the final day against Motherwell at Tynecastle, Hearts were one point behind Kilmarnock, while the Lanarkshire team had already flown and were assured of the Championship flag.

First Division Table

	Played	Won	Drawn	Lost	Points
Motherwell	38	25	9	4	59
Hearts	38	21	8	9	50
Kilmarnock	38	16	17	5	49

That deciding day turned out to be a major let-down as Hearts' stretched squad were forced to reflect on what might have been while Motherwell, with experienced players like Brian McLaughlin, Brian McClair and Willie Irvine, led in such an exhilarating way to the Championship by David Hay, went on to record a second 3-0 win at Tynecastle.

As is so often the case in hindsight, perhaps the delay of a return to the Premier Division was a blessing in disguise. Certainly, the fledgling Mackay, just making his way into the team as a regular, was under no illusions. He reflected, 'After all the comings and goings at the club during the previous nine months, in some ways getting so close might have been an achievement, for our lack of a squad in depth was exposed in the closing weeks. Perhaps we would have been ill-equipped to contend with the Premier Division, and although desperately disappointing at the time, it probably left us in better shape for the following year.'

As if that disappointment was not enough to cope with, Mercer had to reflect on his first year's experience in football, which now contained a deepening financial crisis and, during the second half of the Motherwell game, a terracing problem which would also have to be urgently addressed.

'Three policemen were injured during the fights on that day, and a number of supporters arrested. But I still recall to this day that malicious mischief was not the driving force behind the incidents,' said Mercer. 'It was a desperate desire on the part of the supporters to see their team succeed, and their one way of saying to the people in charge . . . "You have let us down". It was up to me to put that right.

'There was a point when I sat down amid the financial cost of failing to be promoted and the dreadful problems caused by the terracing troubles that the words of my wife the previous summer haunted my mind. "You must be mad to get involved," she had said.'

Although there was never any suggestion that Mercer would walk away from the stricken club, it was time to weigh the pros and cons and look to start again. Little wonder, though, that he was able to take a quiet moment aside to himself and think . . . 'What have you done this time, Mercer?'

MacDonald was, of course, about to provide many of the answers with his shrewd dealings in the transfer market, for his stocktaking had included a clear view that a particular type of player was now needed to take Hearts back into the top flight and the first steps toward the very real progress that manifests itself in the position of the club now.

MacDonald recalled, 'Bringing players to the club in those days was like shopping incessantly from a Littlewoods' catalogue. A pound down and a pound a week was the game we were in, and the item at the top of my shopping list was experience.

'The nucleus of young players was already at the club, and what we needed were men who had been over the course before to lead the youngsters through the task. It was in the preparation for the next two or three years that "Dad's Army" was born.'

Mercer's indelible mark on Hearts, and Scottish football, had now been made and, as is the case today, his style of leadership brought enemies. He is a man who is not in business to be popular, but is involved in whatever sphere of life he selects, at any given time, to succeed. His introduction to the game north of the border has certainly tempted others of his kind into the sport. Would Lawrence Marlborough and later David Murray, and the present Dundee Chairman, Angus Cook, all have followed his path had the Mercer experience not been of such a high-profile nature?

Ego is, of course, an element of his involvement that he does not deny. Over the years, however, his public posture has been able to surround much happier times than in that demanding first season. However, one thing remains constant throughout Mercer's eight years in football, and will be unchanged for as long as he decides to stay involved in football. Life with the Hearts chairman may be many things, but it is never dull.

CHAPTER THREE

Willie Johnston
1982-83

WHEN ALEX MacDonald and Sandy Jardine were looking for a good guy, there was much surprise in Scottish football circles when they selected most people's idea of the perfect bad guy - Willie Johnston.

As the Hearts management team attempted to bridge the generation gap between the young, promising players and the more experienced brigade, they spotted the need for mature men who would be accepted in the dressing-room by impressionable minds. Johnston, they knew from their Rangers and Scotland days, had all the playing credentials but they had an insight into the man who many had not been privy to. Willie had been a tremendous listener and learner, and MacDonald knew that he had the personality and the will to pass the knowledge on.

As a player, Johnston was never far removed from problems. His record reads like everything the SFA have attempted to rectify in recent years. But most of his indiscretions involved retaliations against over physical attention, and not instigations of on-field violence by himself.

The Scotland player's sentences spanned three different disciplinary codes. For some of his first sendings off, the bans were for one month at a time, but the authorities then changed the system to include an escalating period of suspension which was given in games, and then eventually arrived at match bans. Between 1969 and 1974 he had been dismissed against Bilbao and suspended for one month and there were three successive sendings off against Clyde, Hibs and Partick Thistle which involved spiralling sentences of 21 days, 42 days and 63 days respectively. By the mid-Seventies, with West Bromwich, the football authorities had progressed to suspensions which were expressed in the number of games to be missed. Banishments against Swindon,

Everton and Bristol City were expressed in terms of four matches each. Even referees did not escape the Johnston retribution. He was stood down for five matches in October 1976 after a match between West Bromwich and Brighton for allegedly aiming a kick at the match official Derek Lloyd.

The man who now welcomes regulars into the Portbrae Bar in Kirkcaldy's High Street will never be allowed to forget his undignified departure from the World Cup in 1978, when a drug test found traces of stimulants he did not know had been placed on a banned list. Argentina was not one of his favourite world destinations since, one year before the 1978 finals, he had been sent off in a preparation match against the home side.

It was against all that background that Alex MacDonald knew Willie Johnston could be a valuable contributor at Tynecastle.

He joined Hearts in September 1982, but his journey from Ibrox to Edinburgh carried the 35-year-old winger ten thousand miles. Rangers' manager at the time, John Greig, had no need to keep him as a player, but was still sufficiently aware of his potential that he would not allow him to join another Scottish club. The route to Hearts, therefore, was via a summer with the Vancouver Whitecaps on the west coast of Canada and it was not until his season there had finished that Willie was able to accept Hearts' offer of continued involvement at the highest level.

The Tynecastle team was still in Division One but, with a few refinements, MacDonald and Jardine were convinced that a return to the Premier Division could be achieved, and Johnston would add a touch of international class on the pitch and crucial maturity off it in the search for progress.

MacDonald, who had been grappling with the eternal problem of finding improvement within a limited budget, knew through first-hand experience that Johnston's good training habits could still make him capable of contributing, even at the ripe old age of 35.

'There was never any doubt in my mind that Willie would do what we needed of him. He had always done the training, without skipping anything, and above all else he still had a burning desire to keep playing. That's what we needed,' he recalled. 'And his influence off the pitch was impossible to over-estimate. He'd been everywhere and won everything and if there was anyone who could point a new generation of players in the right direction, it was Willie Johnston.

'As a manager I couldn't be everywhere with the players,

Willie Johnston at home with Hearts

particularly when they go out as a group to represent the club, and we were very fortunate with the type of players we had at Tynecastle. But a good influence away from the ground was crucial. Just one raised eyebrow from Willie or later, Jimmy Bone, was enough to tell a player that the horseplay had gone far enough and it was time to settle down again. These two professionals were the link between the club and the players.'

With 22 caps and a vast array of winners' medals, the former Scotland player soon became a firm favourite with the players and, more importantly, the fans, and from less than three-quarters

Star pupil – Gary Mackay

of that first season, he would collect six goals.

The season, without Johnston, had started well.

Sheffield United came to Tynecastle in the first week of August and were beaten 4-2 in a pre-season friendly when Gary Mackay scored twice and Walter Kidd and Dave Bowman, one each. MacKay and Bowman, together with John Robertson, were to be the three players in which Johnston would see Hearts' future.

Three days later, on 7 August in another friendly, an own goal was enough to see Hearts defeat Leeds United 1-0, before Jackie McNamara scored the only goal in the Hibs victory for the Tom Hart Memorial Trophy. From that encouraging pre-season, however, the Tynecastle team moved straight into a first game League Cup defeat. Derek O'Connor managed one goal at Motherwell, but the section matches started off with a 2-1 defeat.

O'Connor was the man on target in the second League Cup tie of the season four days later, when he scored twice in the 2-1 win against Forfar that would go some way to earning consolation for the earlier, infamous Scottish Cup defeat by the Angus team. Forfar's scorer that night was a former Hearts player, Stuart Porter.

There was more good goal news when Hearts completed the first run of League Cup section matches at Shawfield on the Saturday with their most convincing victory of the season. Willie Pettigrew scored four goals and the 7-1 victory was completed with the efforts by Bowman, Peter Shields and a Jim Brogan own goal for Clyde. And progress into the later stages of the competition looked distinctly possible at Station Park on 25 August when Hearts defeated Forfar 2-0 with manager MacDonald and Peter Marinello grabbing the goals. MacDonald was on target again against Motherwell in a 1-0 victory.

The League Cup section games were completed at home against Clyde in another comfortable victory over the Glasgow team, when Shields, Pettigrew and Bowman goals were responsible for the final 3-0 score-line.

The encouragement and confidence from that run in the season's first competition was carried into the start of the league programme at Hampden Park when Marinello and Bowman finished off the hard work in a 2-1 victory. As Hearts waited for Johnston to become free of the Canadian season, there was a tremendous lift in the first leg of the League Cup quarter-final tie against St Mirren at Love Street. Alan Logan scored for Saints but Pettigrew's goal for the Edinburgh team in the away leg would surely count for more in the long run.

The League Cup, and the victories in it, had presented Hearts with a tremendous tonic at such an early stage of the season, but promotion had always been the first, and only, priority and there followed three draws in a week that would seem frustrating but still valuable at the end of the season. Ayr United had Mike Larnach as their scorer at Tynecastle on 11 September but Derek O'Connor continued his consistency near goal to earn a point and, four days later at Muirton Park, Perth, that other free scorer Willie Pettigrew saw Derek Addison, who had moved to the Perth team, cancel out his goal. The third successive 1-1 draw was played out at Brockville and O'Connor was once again the hit-man against Falkirk. The following mid-week would see the chance to overcome St Mirren in the League Cup and earn a place in the semi-final.

The Paisley team had an expert chance-taker in Billy Stark but, with Johnston coming on from the sub-bench to replace Stuart McLaren, Hearts were given a timely lift. MacDonald and Pettigrew counted for the Tynecastle team, and Stark's goal for St

Mirren could not halt their progress.

The League programme continued in a positive way with Bowman's single goal being enough to account for Clyde at home, and then Pettigrew, O'Connor, Pat Byrne and a Sandy Jardine penalty were far too much for Gerry Ronald's reply from Clydebank. Then, going into October, Colin Harris, a player who was later to face Hearts in Edinburgh derbies, would score the only goal of the game against Raith Rovers at Starks Park where Johnston was making a return to his home town.

The financial restraints that had dogged the club during the early part of the decade continued to restrict and frustrate, and Johnston's first impression on rejoining his former Rangers' colleagues, MacDonald and Jardine, was that he had made a major error.

'It was a disaster. I thought I'd made the wrong move but it didn't take long for me to realise that with the young players Hearts had at the time, there would be an enjoyable and satisfying role for me at Tynecastle,' he recalled. 'I knew that's what Doddy wanted me for. I quickly established a relationship with the younger players and in no time at all we were able to establish a really good team spirit at the club.

'At West Brom, under Johnnie Giles, we had always been encouraged to go out as a group for a beer after matches, and everyone had their chance to give an opinion on what had gone right, or wrong, in the match just finished. After a few weeks we would get 12 or 13 of the players coming out with us for a couple of pints and, although we had great fun, at the end of the night it would all get back to football.

'Basically, with Jimmy Bone, who joined us the next year, I hope we convinced the youngsters like Gary, John and David that it was best to be listeners. That's the way we had learned to observe the good habits of the older professionals at Rangers and make sure that we got as close to their way of conducting themselves as we could. We had experience of the mistakes that can be made and we tried to point out to them that they shouldn't repeat them. I know, looking at some of them now, that what we were trying at that time has worked.'

One thing Johnston knew for sure was that the First Division venues that Hearts were visiting each week were not places to relish. His experience had taken him to some of the finest arenas in the world and he was anxious that the Hearts players should follow him. Little did he know at that time that the youngsters he had taken under his wing would be playing in the Olympic Stadium in Munich, and the famous Pratter Stadium, Vienna, and other far-flung destinations before the decade was ended.

'That season I tried to make it clear to the kids that going to the likes of Alloa and Dumbarton, no disrespect to these clubs in particular, was something to put in the past,' he added. 'Some of the grounds we went to in the First Division didn't have enough hot water for everyone to wash in after the match. I always made sure I was quickly into the dressing-room in order to avoid a cold shower.' To his credit, Willie has never used that as an excuse for the 20 sendings off that punctuated his career.

Not that coming to Hearts completely ended his disciplinary problems, for he was in hot water in March 1983 in a Scottish Cup tie at Celtic Park. The SFA were concerned that he had head-butted Davie Proven, but Willie's version that included a 'playful slap', seemed to find favour, for he was simply suspended for one game and suggestions that he would be charged with bringing the game into disrepute turned out not to be accurate. The Hearts chairman had an input in the affair as well, with a strongly-worded letter to the authorities that may well have mitigated in the player's favour.

From the defeat at Kirkcaldy, Hearts were held to a 1-1 draw by Dumbarton at Tynecastle, with Derek O'Connor the scorer, and then three days later, again at home, a certain John Robertson scored his first League goal for the club. This was in a 3-0 victory over Alloa when Roddy McDonald and an own goal completed the score-line; Hearts celebrated a further comfortable victory at Hamilton when MacDonald, Byrne and O'Connor earned two more precious promotion points.

After Robertson had made his scoring break-through, it was Willie Johnston's turn on 23 October against Dunfermline when he scored his first goal for Hearts with assistance from O'Connor, Bowman and MacDonald in a 4-1 Tynecastle win against Dunfermline.

All the early season hard work in the League Cup was rewarded the following Wednesday with a semi-final first-leg match against Rangers at Ibrox but, after tremendous performances from Davie Cooper and Jim Bett, it confirmed Rangers' position as favourites to reach the final. There was no doubt though that the energy expended in Glasgow took its toll in the next League match, when

Derek O'Connor – danger for Dunfermline

John Flood was the chief mischief-maker with two goals for Airdrie at Tynecastle in a 4-2 away victory that saw O'Connor and Sandy Jardine produce Hearts' retaliation.

There was another fine display against Rangers in the second leg of the semi-final going into November but Derek O'Connor's goal could not overcome a Jim Bett penalty and a second from Derek Johnstone as Rangers qualified for Hampden with a 4-1 aggregate.

Johnston was a regular in the starting line-up and took great encouragement from the continued progress of the young players at the club, two of whom, Mackay and Robertson, were scorers in a fine 3-0 away win at Clydebank where O'Connor was also once again on target. As Hearts' position in the promotion race strengthened, there were two further points tucked away from the Tynecastle match against Falkirk where Robertson, with two goals, and Johnston emerged as the main men in a 3-1 win before the team took on the might of Dynamo Kiev, and learned much in a 2-0 defeat.

The promotion push then travelled to Boghead where Derek O'Connor was the marksman for Hearts and Ray Blair, Dumbarton's goal scorer in a 1-1 draw before Johnston's penalty helped

Aerial power of Roddy McDonald and Willie Pettigrew against Raith Rovers

engineer the defeat of his home-town team, Raith Rovers, at Tynecastle, where Gary Mackay scored the other goal in the 2-0 win.

There were five goals at Shawfield, where Hearts just edged out Clyde 3-2 with Pettigrew scoring twice and Alex MacDonald the other in front of another important away win at Ayr. Pettigrew, O'Connor and MacDonald fashioned a 3-0 victory at Somerset Park and then, on New Year's Day, Pettigrew again drove in the goal that defeated St Johnstone.

The former Motherwell and Dundee United player was in the midst of a tremendous spell and his single goal against Airdrie in Lanarkshire was enough for victory on 3 January, before he shared the scoring responsibility with Derek O'Connor at home to Hamilton in a 2-1 win. There were no goals at all on 15 January at Recreation Park, Alloa, and no goals for Hearts at Tynecastle one week later when Donald Park was Partick Thistle's match-winner.

Scottish Cup time came round at the end of January when Hearts were happy to earn a replay from a trip to Dumfries where Peter Shields scored the goal that cancelled out Jim Robertson's effort for the Borders team. Derek O'Connor settled that argument in the replay at Tynecastle but, after a free Saturday, the League points were left behind in Dunfermline when Roddy McDonald headed a goal that was overtaken by efforts from Bobby Forrest and Grant Jenkins.

All that was forgotton at Tynecastle when Hearts hit the net five times against Ayr United, thanks to five individual scorers. O'Connor, Pettigrew, Mackay, Bowman and Byrne all indicated that Alex MacDonald was starting to assemble a team that contained goals in every department.

A place in the Scottish Cup quarter-finals was earned in the fourth round at Tynecastle against East Fife, when Roddy McDonald and O'Connor overtook a Martin Caithness goal for the Fife team, and then, in the league, John Robertson claimed his first hat-trick in the first 3-0 win at Queen's Park. That was followed by a home set-back in a 2-1 defeat by Falkirk when O'Connor was the scorer, and Willie Johnston's dismissal did not help against Celtic in the Cup tie at Celtic Park, when Alex MacDonald provided Hearts' only reply in a 4-1 defeat.

Another Robertson hat-trick was the feature of a 4-0 home win against Partick Thistle and he was joined by Mackay and Roddy McDonald in a 3-1 victory over Clyde, again at Tynecastle.

Starks Park held disappointment again in the final week of March when the former Hearts player, Colin More, was one of Raith Rovers' scorers in the Fife team's 4-2 defeat where Johnston's goal-haul was assisted by two successful penalty kicks. There was another penalty at Airdrie four days later, converted by Mackay, and Robertson weighed in with the second goal in a 2-0 victory. Then Robbo and Gerry McCabe scored two goals each at Tynecastle in a drawn match against Clydebank.

As the race for a place in the Premier Division continued to be dominated by St Johnstone, Hearts and Clydebank, a point from Alloa seemed reasonable thanks to Alex MacDonald's goal; there was no defeat either against Dunfermline in the third-last fixture of the season, when John Robertson scored his third hat-trick in a 3-3 draw.

Promotion to the Premier Division was clinched in the opening two weeks of May when Robertson hit two goals and O'Connor and Mackay one each in a 4-0 drubbing of Dumbarton, and on the final day at a joyous Tynecastle, Willie Johnston had the pleasure of sharing the goals with Derek O'Connor in the 2-0 defeat of Hamilton. That was fitting, for there can be no doubt that his playing influence in that crucial season for Hearts is impossible to over estimate. But in bringing him from Canada, MacDonald had introduced an influence that is still with the club today.

It is not possible to hold a conversation with anyone at Tynecastle for more than five minutes without a Willie Johnston or Jimmy Bone story being told. And is not difficult to spot that the marvellous spirit which has been such a Trojan ally to Hearts over the years owes much to the Johnston influence.

'I thoroughly enjoyed the final couple of years in my career with Hearts, and had it not been such a good time I would have finished playing earlier. I had always promised myself that the minute the fun went out of it I would stop, and that's eventually what I did,' said Johnston.

'The one disappointment for me, in common with others, has been that Hearts have been unable to win a trophy that their play deserves. They have been so close so many times, but there is a prize in them, and I am sure they will pick it up.'

As the players, under manager Joe Jordan, set about that task, every Hearts player who was present during Willie Johnston's input will be unanimous: they will want him there when the presentation is made.

CHAPTER FOUR

Jimmy Bone
1983-84

JIMMY BONE'S recruitment to Tynecastle was shrouded in the stuff of the great Hollywood thriller. As he made his way into the baggage reclaim area in Glasgow Airport, after a spell with Hong Kong Rangers, there was a mysterious tannoy announcement.

'Do not do anything until you have spoken to me,' read the scrawled message at the Information Desk. The signatory to the note was, of course, manager Alex MacDonald . . . and it had been the call Bone was waiting for. Freed by St Mirren at the end of the previous season, one of Scotland's most respected strikers had spent the summer in the Far East mulling over several offers. The problem with most of them was that, at the age of 34, the majority were for coaching jobs which did not involve playing.

'I was due to meet Hibs' manager, Pat Stanton, and chairman, Kenny Waugh, but like so many people Pat wanted to offer me a coaching position with no prospect of turning out for the first team,' he explained.

'Okay, age was against me in the Premier Division but the problem was conveying to anyone interested that I genuinely felt able to contribute at that level. The summer in the blistering heat of Hong Kong had my weight right, and I felt as good as ever.

'Before I got to the stage of talking to Alex and Sandy, I had virtually pleaded with Pat Stanton to include playing as part of the Hibs' deal but, in fairness to Pat, he had his ideas for the future, and my part in them was in the backroom staff. That was why Alex's offer was perfect for me, for they had a young man called John Robertson firing in goals every week, and as well as making my own contribution to the team, they could perhaps see me as someone who could bring John on as well.

'I had always been a good listener as a player, and have never had any doubt in my ability to pass it on, so really the job of

Bone's fine finish – against Rangers

helping Hearts to consolidate in the Premier Division, at such an important time for the club, was tailor-made.'

Bone was then, and still is, a tremendous joker so in that aspect too he was the perfect man for Hearts. MacDonald and Jardine had no money to spend, in any great volume, but that did not stop them vetting very carefully the type of professional they were bringing to Tynecastle. The unique spirit in the dressing-room that still earns results from indifferent performances was starting to develop and in players like Bone, and before him, Willie Johnston, the Hearts management team had recruited rare material. Both had experience at the very highest level, and were still capable of injecting their moments of magic in a game without the need to do the running around that the more tender elements of the team could provide. It was around this time that the description, 'Dad's Army', was beginning to be coined and really that was no great mystery. In addition to Bone, 35 on his birthday in September, Johnston would be 37 towards Christmas time. MacDonald, who was becoming the first player/manager ever in the Premier Division, had recently turned 35 . . . nine months and two weeks older than his assistant manager, Sandy Jardine, who, of course, is a rare 'Hogmanay Baby'.

At the other end of the spectrum, of course, were 19-year-olds Dave Bowman, Paul Cherry, Gary Mackay, new signing Malcolm Murray and John Robertson. In years to come, the task facing Jardine and MacDonald was to successfully fill in the gap between their older, experienced players and the group possessing all the future potential.

'That was why players like Jimmy were so important to us at the time,' said MacDonald. 'We didn't have the finance to compete for the players in that middle age group, so we shopped around and selected the right types very carefully. We had to find mature players who were interested enough to spend time and energy on the younger men.

'The Jimmy Bones of this world were not quick buck merchants, indeed I'm sure he could have had a better paid job in coaching, elsewhere. But when we made contact with him it was clear he was desperate to play. We had to have players with that hunger if we were to steer the team through what was undoubtedly going to be an exceptionally difficult season back in the top division.'

Bone chose Hearts and, having roomed with Sandy Jardine on Scotland Under-23 business and played against many of the Hearts' first team squad, would have no difficulty in settling in. However, there were ground rules that he was to appreciate very early on.

He joined the Hearts' touring party on a pre-season trip up north and, having booked into the hotel, he quickly made contact with 'Bud' Johnston in order that the pair might have a small beer in Inverness to celebrate their re-established friendship.

Capital Press

OFFICIAL PHOTOGRAPHER TO HEART OF MIDLOTHIAN F.C.

35 SOUTH TRINITY ROAD
EDINBURGH EH5 3PN
TEL: 031-552 3450

It's a derby treat – for John Robertson

A taxi was hailed, but the management team intelligence service had been working ahead of them, and when they jumped into the car at the front door there was a nasty shock waiting in the back seat. MacDonald and Jardine had plugged in to their taxi request and thought it only fair they should oblige their senior players. 'You are fined a week's wages, Jimmy,' said MacDonald. 'Now you can come and have a beer with us and we'll explain to you what we need at Tynecastle this season.'

'All I could do was hold my hands up and plead guilty,' admitted Bone. 'I had been wrong and Alex was quite right. That's the sort of no-nonsense, but scrupulously fair discipline that has made Hearts the club they are today.'

There were other new players recruited that summer, but gone were the days when big money could be brandished around in the search for improvement . . . indeed these were the days when no money could be brandished around.

Donald Park returned from Partick Thistle for his second spell at the club, having previously been at Tynecastle between 1972 and 1978 and his adaptability, performing as he could in midfield and up front, would be a useful option. Another important factor was that he was only 30.

But the directors were also able to go into the market as spenders, although the long and serious negotiations for the transfer of Malcolm Murray seemed positively comical compared with the type of transactions that Hearts can involve themselves in now. The 18-year-old from Buckie had been down with Leicester City in England where their manager, Jock Wallace - 'Doddy's' boss at Ibrox and long-term friend - had a tremendous intelligence network.

'We went to see him play in a match at Hampden against Queen's Park and had to think long and hard about Buckie Thistle's valuation of £2,000 for a player that the manager reckoned had good potential at right back,' recollected Wallace Mercer. 'In the end we settled on £1,000, and agreed to play a match up at Buckie as a compromise. But the arguments we had over that money are still to this day a sobering memory and a reminder of just how far we've come in the meantime.'

Another new recruit was George Cowie, another former Buckie Thistle player who was joining Hearts from West Ham, having been surprisingly given a free transfer. Five years previously, George captained the Scottish Youth Team of his day and Upton Park manager George Lyall was disappointed that a player that he had a high opinion of had rarely pushed forward past the fringe of the West Ham first team. His loss was Hearts' gain for in subsequent years George went on to be a valuable contributor at Tynecastle, though he had his playing career cruelly interrupted after a move to Dunfermline. Hearts were to participate in a major way to George's Testimonial in Fife later.

With Donald Park born in Inverness and Roddy McDonald hailing from Dingwall, there was no shortage of Highland blood in the Hearts team setting out once again into the rigours of the Premier Division, so it was fitting that the whole procedure should begin up north.

The first match of the Highland tour, against Nairn County, was to provide the perfect start to the season with eight goals being placed in the Highland League side's net. David Bowman, Roddy McDonald and Donald Park scored twice, while Gary Mackay and the gaffer himself completed the scoring. Jimmy Bone then made his début on 3 August in Inverness, against Caley, and the 2-0 defeat by one of the north's strongest sides was the perfect reminder that nothing could be taken for granted in the long months ahead. However, the three-match sequence was completed

The meat in the sandwich is Gary Mackay

against Elgin City where Cowie scored the only goal of the match in front of his family to send the tourists back to Edinburgh for even stiffer tasks against Leeds United and Leicester City before the Premier Division season would get underway against St Johnstone at Perth.

Gary Mackay, David Bowman and Ian Westwater had earlier in the year performed for Scotland in the World Youth Championships in Mexico, but John Robertson was to create something of a controversy in a Scotland Youth match down south. Scotland were losing 4-0 to England in the Under-18 European Championships when John was introduced as a substitute, and in his usual inimitable style proceeded to score two goals. However, they will never appear in the very extensive list of Robertson goals. At that time, international youth football was outwith the reach of any player who had already performed in a league match, and as Robbo featured in the first team against Hamilton he was deemed ineligible for the tournament.

In the pre-season games against the English clubs, Henry Smith was delighted once again to keep a clean sheet in the 0-0 draw against his former club, Leeds, and although Robertson's goals against England had been in vain his two against Leicester City were legitimate, if not sufficient to avoid a 3-2 defeat.

So it was on to Muirton Park and the opening Premier Division fixture, and how fitting that a spectacular Jimmy Bone goal should start the League campaign in perfect style with a single-goal victory that contained with it an interesting statistic. It was the first time that Hearts had started a campaign in the Premier Division with a victory. In the previous four years they had lost to Hibs, drawn and lost against Aberdeen, and in the relegation season of 1980/81 commenced with a 3-2 defeat by Partick Thistle. At the end of a long and arduous campaign the two points in Perth would be crucial in hoisting Hearts into the top half of the table and into Europe.

A double header against Cowdenbeath followed in the League Cup and, after a 0-0 draw at Central Park, Gary Mackay scored the goal at Tynecastle which saw the teams finish 1-1. Hearts won the penalty shoot-out 4-2. Yes, they were a factor in the game even before the World Cup in Italy!

Love Street, Paisley, was the venue in the next round of the League Cup competition and a feature of that match would be the goal scorers. The match finished square at 2-2 but Jimmy Bone and John Robertson were the men on target, names that were to punctuate the goal scoring sheets for the rest of the season.

The first Edinburgh derby at Tynecastle followed, and it was the first time the teams had met in the League since March 1979 when Willie Gibson scored Hearts' goal in the 2-1 defeat. This time the outcome was different when, seemingly inevitably, Bone and Robertson were the hit men again. Robbo claimed two of the three goals in the 3-2 victory. Oddly, two players who also did duty at Tynecastle, Ralph Callachan and Willie Irvine, were the Hibs' scorers in that first derby of the Eighties. The Hearts line-up that day was Henry Smith, Stuart Gauld and George Cowie; Sandy Jardine, Roddy McDonald, Stewart McLaren; Dave Bowman, John Robertson, Jimmy Bone (sub Willie Johnston), Donald Park and Gary Mackay (sub Alex MacDonald).

The next week saw two meetings against Rangers which contained vastly differing fortunes. In the first, a League Cup-tie, the Ibrox team went home comfortable 3-0 winners, but when they returned on League duty four days later, things were to be very different. In the midweek match injury had taken its toll but by Saturday Walter Kidd, John Robertson, Jimmy Bone and Stewart McLaren were all available and included for the weekend fixture. The 3-1 scoreline tells it all. The whole composition of the team looked much more comfortable, and goals by Alex MacDonald, Bowman and Robertson earned two more crucial points against a side which included a young man ready to break through into the first team . . . Dave McPherson.

After a team containing a mixture of youth and experience was beaten 2-0 by Berwick Rangers in the East of Scotland Shield, Roddy McDonald once again illustrated his value when pushed forward by scoring the only goal of the match against St Mirren in Paisley.

By that time, although the chilly, gloomier nights of October had not yet arrived, Bone was making an incredible contribution to the season. He had scored in the club's first four League matches, becoming the first Hearts player to achieve such a feat. Into the bargain, he and John Robertson had four goals each to show for their efforts, despite the blank week at Love Street, and were joined by the following names at the top of the Premier Division scoring list, all on four: Billy Kirkwood (Dundee United), Mark McGhee (Aberdeen), John Brogan (St Johnstone) and Celtic's Tommy Burns and Brian McClair.

Then came a disappointing sequence of six matches without a victory, although three of them - against Clydebank in the League Cup, together with Motherwell and Celtic in the Championship - were draws. Donald Park scored against Clydebank and 'Boney' at Parkhead. Sandwiching these draws was a home defeat by

The eyes have it against Celtic

Aberdeen and a 1-0 reverse at Tannadice, both in the League, and the return League Cup match against Rangers which saw the tables turned in the Ibrox team's favour, the result 2-0.

St Johnstone visited Tynecastle on the final day of October and the slump was ended with a 2-0 victory, the second against the Perth team in the season, with John Robertson scoring twice to end suggestions that the goals were drying up. Over at Easter Road the following week, Robbo further confirmed that by netting in a 1-1 draw that typified the very physical and swift nature that the derby fixture had taken on. Understandably, the cost of failure is high.

Derek O'Connor's effort, a penalty from Gary Mackay and yet another Robertson goal were enough to see off St Mirren at Tynecastle in the League as mid-November neared, and Mackay was on target again from the spot on an unlucky 13th, as Dundee travelled back to Dens with two points, thanks to a 3-1 victory.

The twice-annual trek to Aberdeen followed the week after, when 4,000 Hearts fans swelled the crowd to almost 20,000, but there was no joy at Pittodrie in a tremendous match that the Dons finally won 2-0.

Having been drawn against St Mirren in the League Cup, matches against the Paisley side were becoming too common a feature and the teams played a 2-2 draw at Tynecastle, with Gary Mackay scoring both goals when careless errors cost the victory . . . and then Robertson scored twice and Willie Johnston once in a 3-0 League Cup victory against Clydebank.

Rangers also had been far too regular opponents in the opening months of the season and, in the first week in December, a 3-0 defeat at Ibrox marked the poorest performance of the season so far. The consolation in the match was a fine début performance by Craig Levein, who had not yet enjoyed the fruits of full-time training.

Levein had been watched by virtually every top club, both north and south of the border, while he was with Cowdenbeath. He had joined them in 1981 from Lochore Welfare and his 60 appearances for the Fife club had quickly made him one of the hottest properties in Scotland. But while many other managers wanted just one more look, MacDonald and Jardine were convinced that they had seen one of the brightest prospects around, and of course time has proved that to be one of the smartest examples of judgement this decade.

Dundee United were Tynecastle's next visitors and the 0-0 draw indicated just how awkward they were as opponents, having broken through the stranglehold that Rangers, Celtic and Aberdeen had held on the major prizes in domestic football.

The well-established scoring trend continued over Christmas, with Robertson scoring Hearts' only goal in a 3-1 defeat by Celtic at Tynecastle and Jimmy Bone earning a Boxing Day draw against Motherwell at Fir Park. The year ended with yet another Muirton Park victory, courtesy of Donald Park and George Cowie in a 2-1 win. By the turn of the year John Robertson, having turned 19 in October, had helped himself to 11 competitive goals while his front-line partner, Bone, had weighed in with seven. At that tender age, given everything that is said about the Premier Division, Robertson's figures were exemplary.

'I have no doubt in saying that John Robertson was the best striker I have ever played with,' insisted Bone. 'He has an in-built antenna which only the very top front players have, that instinctive ability to spot a chance a pace ahead of everyone else.

'Mind you, he had to have his backside booted a few times along

Jimmy Bone - a great pro

the way but I felt, with the relationship we had quickly built up in just a few short months, that I was perhaps one of the best placed to do it. The wee man always had a tendency to put on weight and any time we were out, or perhaps having something to eat pre-match, I would keep one eye on where his hands were. One look and one raised eyebrow were usually enough to stem the temptation.

'I had one favourite trick up my sleeve if I felt at any time he wasn't doing enough off the ball. Before the game I would take John to one side and complain that for me things weren't just right on the day. I would say, "Robbo, I don't know what it is, but I just don't feel a 100 per cent today. Perhaps it's just a touch of a virus, or maybe a little strain, but maybe you could do just a wee bit more than your fair share for this one week."

'It always worked. The wee fella would run around legless that afternoon and of course there was absolutely nothing wrong with me. We really buzzed as a partnership any time I tried that . . . but of course it lost its value if done too often.

'I've been absolutely delighted to see that John's starting to break into the Scotland set-up, and I'm sure it's only a matter of time, even if he has a fair bit of leeway to make up in terms of experience at full cap level, that he establishes himself among the best,' forecast Bone.

'The one thing that is unique about strikers as far as opinions are concerned, and everyone has plenty of them to offer, is tangible evidence. Over the seasons, John Robertson's scoring record stands ready for scrutiny by the best. . . he does it year in year out.

'When I think back to the happy times at Tynecastle, I realise just how much of a thrill it was to play with him and, of course, the many other fine, young men that were brought forward and groomed in preparation for one of the most physical leagues in the world. There was so much fun about the place, certainly in the dressing-room, but even right up to boardroom level, where in a way that you didn't find anywhere else, there was a bond between everyone - they were all doing their best for Hearts.'

Jimmy Bone certainly does not lack experience in terms of geography to make comparisons between the Edinburgh club and others. He has served Partick Thistle, Norwich City, Sheffield United, Celtic, Arbroath, St Mirren, Toronto Blizzards and Hong Kong Rangers as an out and out player. Hearts thought so much of him when he moved back to Gayfield to be player/manager that Wallace Mercer placed a first option on his next move, which was to take him back to another of his former clubs, St Mirren, as assistant to Alex Smith. Then, after the pair had led the Paisley team to a remarkable Scottish Cup triumph, both men went their separate ways. . . Smith to Aberdeen and Bone as assistant manager to Dundee United, before Jimmy was given the chance to be his own man again, as manager of Airdrie.

Hearts 5000th goal, for Jimmy Bone at Tannadice

Even now he recalls the journey back to Edinburgh, from a pre-season tour up north, when Wallace Mercer sat with him at the back of the coach and had a long chat. 'That's the kind of togetherness that rules at the club, and makes it different to any other I've been with.'

The weather intervened in the opening weeks of the New Year, but not enough to halt the derby match going ahead at Tynecastle when Donald Park was the Hearts scorer in 1-1 draw which saw Craig Levein taste the Hibs fixture for the first time. Then on 7 January a disastrous 4-1 defeat by Dundee had John Robertson back on the goal trail by way of some recompense. Gary Mackay missed a penalty on a forgettable day.

That was it, until Partick Thistle came to call in the Scottish Cup in the first week of February, but not before the first-team squad had enjoyed a four-day training break in Marbella, which was not only a perfectly sound idea but an indication that the club's finances were going in the right direction also.

The break certainly seemed to have done the trick as far as the Cup was concerned, and Bone and George Cowie scored the goals that mattered for Hearts to earn a crack at Dundee United in the fourth round, although ground advantage for Jim McLean's team saw them through 2-1. Robertson, from the penalty spot, counted for Hearts. A sending-off for Jimmy Bone early in the second half didn't help.

Between the cup-ties a point had been gleaned from Rangers in a 2-2 Tynecastle draw in the League, which started disastrously but could have finished so sweetly. Down 2-0, to goals from Ally McCoist and Bobby Williamson, Hearts hit back through goals by Derek O'Connor and John Robertson and only the woodwork prevented a Peter Shields drive from completing a memorable comeback.

Brian McClair, fast becoming one of Scotland's most prolific marksmen, was hard on Hearts at the end of February with a hat-trick at Parkhead in a 4-1 defeat in which Donald Park scored the away goal. Celtic's other scorer? John Colquhoun.

John Robertson continued to underline Jimmy Bone's assessment against Motherwell, scoring both Hearts' goals in a 2-1 Tynecastle victory before Walter Kidd had Hearts in the lead at Tannadice in a bid to avenge the Cup defeat. United's 3-1 scoreline hardly reflected the way the match had evolved.

Willie Johnston brought a smile to the school end with Hearts' goal in a 1-1 draw with St Mirren and then the Robertson-Bone partnership won the day a week later, in the reverse fixture at Love Street. Three successive League draws followed against Dundee United, Aberdeen and Rangers as a place in the UEFA Cup for the following season became a real possibility, with some care. The only goals in the three draws were at Pittodrie, where Robertson again was the finisher in a 1-1 scoreline.

Hearts collected a worthwhile scalp in a mid-April friendly against Arsenal, when Kidd, Bone and Mackay found the London side's net in a 3-2 victory which set the players up perfectly to take a vital point from their final meeting with city rivals, Hibs, at Easter Road.

All that was needed for a return to Europe was to avoid defeats, and goals from Donald Park and Roddy McDonald against St Johnstone at home ensured a point in a 2-2 draw, although Aberdeen were to cause a flutter or two with Stewart McKimmie's goal at Tynecastle in the first week of May. However, in the closing three fixtures of the season, Willie Johnston cancelled out a Tommy Burns goal against Celtic, Gary Mackay's effort earned a point at Dens Park and, fittingly, a John Robertson penalty at Fir Park on the final day ended the season with a victory.

Incredibly, in July in Switzerland, Hearts would be going into the draw for the UEFA Cup after their return to the top league in Scotland. It was an achievement that astounded and delighted Wallace Mercer.

'Coming into the season, everyone at the club was set on establishing ourselves in the top league. With two of the ten teams relegated, the casualty rate is high and simply to avoid Division One would have been regarded as a success,' he said. 'Although Europe will represent a tremendous challenge for our players, the chance to compete on this wider stage is a marvellous reward for a season of tremendous commitment, which reflects the work put in by everyone at Tynecastle.'

After winning the friendly at Buckie which accompanied young Malcolm Murray's move to Hearts, there was just one occasion left before the curtain came down on a memorable season . . . a Testimonial match for Alex MacDonald. There was only one club that could realistically provide the opposition for such a match – the team he served so unswervingly since he moved to Ibrox from St Johnstone for £50,000 in 1968 – Rangers.

Kevin Keegan, who had just finished his English League career at Newcastle, travelled north to complete a fitting tribute. John Robertson and Gary Mackay scored as Rangers won 3-2 . . . but no one cared.

As for Jimmy Bone, his first year at Hearts had been a season of tremendous achievement and, although he would soon be on his travels, his part in the Eighties story is not forgotten. 'Jimmy Bone's influence in his time at the club was priceless, it's as simple as that,' praised MacDonald.

CHAPTER FIVE

Gary Mackay
1984-85

THE SEASON when Aberdeen won the Premier Division Championship by seven points from Celtic, with the rest of the teams strung out, right down to Morton with only five victories and two draws to show from their 36 games, may seem an odd period in which to emphasise Gary Mackay's input at Hearts for more than a decade.

Indeed, he missed much of the season, having sustained a broken bone in his foot and, having recovered from that, spectated again late in the campaign when the injury recurred.

But for Mackay, Dave Bowman – who was to move to Coventry in December – and John Robertson, it truly was a time when the youngsters recruited by Bobby Moncur had quickly to take on adult responsibility, in a team often criticised for being soft in the middle generation. The Dad's Army tag was generally treated with good humour at Tynecastle, but the accusation that Alex MacDonald and Sandy Jardine had not adequately filled the void between the vast experience at Hearts and the raw youth coming through was not.

Although the younger element in the Tynecastle squad were certainly tender in years (Mackay was only 20 at the start of the season), they had already been performing with regularity in the first team and their experience outweighed their youth.

So, in terms of years, Hearts perhaps did look lopsided but the maturity Mackay had gained during the most successful years of Scottish Youth football, at international level and in the Hearts' first team, to a large degree made up for that.

The responsibility was being placed on these young shoulders because the influence of the likes of Jimmy Bone and Willie Johnston was starting to wane and, although that contained no shortage of pressure, Mackay, in hindsight, has no regrets.

He explained, 'Right from the start we were asked to do a lot as teenagers so new demands were not something that made us apprehensive about what was ahead. Although we were thrown in much earlier than many players going through the learning stage, we had the great advantage of having tremendous experience to lean on.

'And right from day one there was a tremendous spirit and atmosphere within the Club, which Alex MacDonald and Sandy Jardine did so much to foster, that going in to Tynecastle in the morning was such a joy, and made the difficult periods so much easier to cope with.

'There were non-stop jokes being played here and there... and Johnston and Bone were usually in the middle of the horseplay, although Dave Bowman from our group was a very quick learner.

'There were occasions when players found their shoes nailed to the dressing room floor and jackets stitched up at the sleeves, which on a Monday morning made even the most depressing defeat two days earlier somehow seem easier to accept.

'Looking back now, it was a device that the management team and the senior pros at the time used to keep the pressure off us. All of my early seasons contained a survival element to a fair degree, so light relief definitely helped us carry the responsibility.

'There were times away at the start when we were uncertain whether there would be a wage packet at the end of the week, and it's only when you reflect on these difficult times that you appreciate what's been done at Hearts over the years and hopefully what will be continued in the future.

'There were so many times in the early seasons when that very individual spirit and comradeship that we had within the side turned a draw or a defeat into victory . . . generally against teams that would be expected to beat us.'

Mackay's father, Peter, and mother, Sandra, who are still a big influence on him, were heavily involved in his decision to choose Tynecastle from virtually every big club in Britain who had seen the Salvesen's Boys Club product as a certain full-time professional of the future.

They had spoken to Manchester United, Celtic, Arsenal, Tottenham and Rangers before the family decided that home would be best for a teenager and that in Bobby Moncur, who was manager in 1980 when the decision was made, was a manager who

The squad - ready for the season

had youth as a priority.

Mackay filled every hope that Moncur had foreseen in his ability during the early years of MacDonald's time in charge, but it was in season 1984/85 that he would finally put all the formative years to the test as a senior player.

It was in late June when Hearts played their first match, up in their accustomed Highland pre-season patch, and there was great personal satisfaction in the opening match against Ross County which saw him score twice, although that was balanced by team disappointment with the 2-2 scoreline.

Seven goals followed against Wick Academy, who could only muster one in reply, before Mackay was on target again in the 5-2 victory over Inverness Clach as the Hearts team that can still be recognised today started to take shape.

Henry Smith, Walter Kidd, Craig Levein, John Robertson and Mackay were all present in the side that finished the trip up north in Elgin with a 2-0 victory. Levein and Kenny Black from the penalty spot scored the goals but the match ended the season for some weeks for Mackay. A broken bone in his foot had been discovered and he would not reappear until mid-September, just four days before Hearts were due to make their return to

European competition against Paris St Germain in the UEFA Cup.

The final pre-season match saw Hearts perform for the first time at home, against difficult English First Division opposition in Queen's Park Rangers, and the 3-2 victory seemed to have set the team up perfectly for a difficult opening away match in the league against Dundee United.

Roddy MacDonald and John Robertson were on target and the result was helped on nicely by an own goal, but it did not assist at Tannadice against Dundee United, where the team went down 2-0 to remind everyone at Tynecastle that the season ahead would contain no shortage of difficult tests.

The following week at home, Brian Whittaker scored against Morton in a match in which a player who was later to turn out for Hearts briefly, Murray McDermott, was to emerge as the key character. Hearts had 80 per cent of the match, but McDermott's acrobatics and the slackness at the back saw Alec O'Hara and Doug Robertson score killer goals.

Goals came aplenty, however, in a League Cup tie against East Stirling the following midweek. With Mackay still absent, the team had four individual scorers in a comfortable victory. Levein, Bone, Johnston and Whittaker were the men who earned an away tie against Ayr United in the next round.

Then it was off to Easter Road for the first derby of the season, and the confidence gained from the part-timers from Falkirk proved decisive. Paul Kane, always such a committed player in the derby match, had Hibs ahead at half time, but Craig Levein helped a Sandy Jardine clearance behind Alan Rough, and Derek O'Connor was the derby hero with a last-minute winner.

Somerset Park in the League Cup was the next venue and Derek O'Connor was again the vital player in the 1-0 victory. A Jimmy Bone cross once again highlighted O'Connor's ability in the air and the Cup run continued, with a home and away tie against Dundee in the Fourth Round to prepare for.

The victories continued, first against Dumbarton in the League, when Donald Park dived to head the winner after 39 minutes at Tynecastle, and then in the League Cup when Park this time was the architect of the separating goal, finished by the trusty head of Roddy MacDonald. Henry Smith was a Dens Park hero that night, with several outstanding late saves.

Five successive wins with only one goal conceded lifted

optimism at Tynecastle, but the worry was that the best performance so far had been contained in Cup matches, and a home League defeat by St Mirren on 8 September mainly confirmed that view.

So many times St Mirren had been surprise winners against Hearts, but after 50 minutes when John Robertson sent in the opening goal from the penalty spot, it looked good for Hearts. However, Brian Gallagher equalised midway through the second half, and then Frank McAvennie drove the winner past Henry Smith ten minutes from time. Not even a sending off for Neil Cooper late in the match could help the team back into contention.

An away game at Parkhead came next, and it hardly seemed the ideal preparation for a return to Europe against the Paris side in the Parc des Princes Stadium. It looked even less appropriate when Brian Whittaker was sent off, having been cautioned twice soon after replacing the injured Walter Kidd. Frank McGarvie completed the gloom with a 58th minute winner.

All of that was forgotten, however, when Hearts travelled back into Europe against the French side, who from their frequent spy missions, the Hearts backroom staff recognised as high quality indeed. The 4-0 home victory put together in the three-tiered national stadium emphasised that opinion.

Even then, the thousands of Hearts fans who made the journey by air, train, coach and car not only thoroughly enjoyed the experience but behaved impeccably at a time when the ability to travel abroad on football matters with some restraint was crucial.

In the Sixties, Hearts had been regular features of both the Inter Cities Fairs Cup and on one occasion the European Cup, but the Seventies had not been nearly so productive.

Seven years before the match in Paris the team had made their one and only appearance in the Cup Winners' Cup, and the opening leg against Locomotiv Leipzig in East Germany had seen Hearts bring back a 2-0 defeat that would surely be difficult to overturn at Tynecastle. However, the aggregate score was level inside an hour, through goals from Roy Kay and Willie Gibson and, although the Germans equalised through Fritche four minutes before the interval, goals from Jimmy Brown, Drew Busby and Gibson again saw the Edinburgh men through by two clear goals.

By the left, in Europe, against Dukla Prague

The second round saw Hearts pitted against higher grade opposition, in West Germany's SV Hamburg, but Busby and Donald Park each scored in the 4-2 away first-leg defeat. Worse was to follow at Tynecastle, when Gibson was the only scorer in a highly impressive 4-1 Hamburg victory. So, after the absence from European club competition the prospect of playing in France was a real highlight, although everyone realised the nature of the task in hand. Mackay had returned in the Celtic defeat, and was delighted to have the opportunity of making his European début. He recalled, 'To this day, Samir Susic, who recently gave Scotland so many problems in the World Cup qualifying matches, is the best player I have played against. It's difficult, because of the talent he possesses, to know whether to describe him as a midfield player or a forward.

'He was 29 the time we played the Paris team, and scored two magnificent goals in the first leg. The first was a superbly struck free kick, and the second a fierce volley from a cross ball, and he even found time later in the match to create the fourth goal for Richard Niedᴄ.bacher.

'They also had a superb entertainer in left winger, Nambatinque Toko, who gave us all sorts of problems in wide positions, and really his trickery and pace summed up our opponents.

'They showed us a completely new dimension in terms of

opposition, but time was to show that they were still some way short of the European winning standard. They were heavily beaten by Videoton of Hungary, who went on to lose in the final to Real Madrid.

'But just playing in that stadium and sampling the atmosphere before nearly 22,000 fans, against what had been France's best supported club the previous season, was a tremendous thrill and indicated to us just how far Hearts had come in a short time.'

There was no doubt that the rigours of midweek in Europe took their toll in the following league match against Dundee at Tynecastle when two players, both with links to Hearts in later years, were Dundee's goal scorers.

John Brown hit the net first after half an hour, and, of course, he was later to be the subject of a £200,000 transfer bid, which collapsed at the last minute following a problem which developed over a medical examination.

The foot injury which Mackay had sustained in the pre-season matches flared again just before half time, but despite Hearts going on to enjoy a good spell in the early part of the second half, Tosh McKinlay, since a first-team regular at Tynecastle, swept in Dundee's second.

The action stayed at Tynecastle, and with Tayside opponents in the following midweek when a drama-packed, controversial match saw Hearts lose the first leg of their League Cup semi-final against Dundee United. John Robertson started the night off in perfect style when he cracked in a first-minute free kick to encourage dreams of a Hampden appearance. Midway through the first half, however, Henry Smith departed with an eye injury, but Dave Bowman – now a United favourite, of course – took over for a brief spell before Henry returned to keep Hearts in front at the interval.

John Clark was the man who turned hopes of victory into defeat, with two headed goals inside four second-half minutes shortly after the interval, but the drama had not ended. Seven players were booked in the match, and in the closing ten minutes, Bowman and Dave Narey were sent off by referee Alan Ferguson.

Later, it was to emerge that Narey would be punished doubly, after words to the referee as he came off the pitch would be treated as a second ordering off offence. With the French side still to meet at home, Hearts then travelled to Aberdeen hoping to avoid a fifth successive Premier Division defeat. The journey was in vain.

The team had coped splendidly in many matches, but the long run in the League Cup and involvement in Europe were clearly taking a heavy toll and, after Sandy Jardine went off injured at Pittodrie, the roof fell in. Four times in the second half Aberdeen scored without reply – the men who did the damage were Frank McDougall (twice), Willie Falconer and Ian Angus.

Still, that did not halt the Tynecastle team from putting on a real show in the second leg of the UEFA Cup match, and despite being down a goal, twice, in the home tie, a 2-2 draw was achieved. Niederbacher and Philippe Jeanol, a defender referred to in France as 'La Classe', twice had the Paris team in front but equalisers from John Robertson, in 27 minutes and 85 minutes, earned Hearts true respectability from the game. The disappointing sequence was broken in satisfying fashion three days later in a 1-0 win over Rangers, when Robertson again was the player with an eye for a goal before the League Cup exit was confirmed at Tannadice in a 3-1 defeat when Donald Park was the consolation scorer. The following Saturday at Tynecastle offered the team the chance to extract revenge from United for the two defeats in the League Cup, and they accepted the chance with real determination. Two goals inside four minutes, before half an hour had been played, first from Park and then Robertson, earned two precious Premier Division points.

During a despondent group of matches in the League, Hearts when embarked on a positive run, encouraged by the victories over Rangers and United, and Morton at Cappielow were the next victims. The visitors won 3-2 with Kenny Black, John Robertson and yet another former Ibrox new boy, Sandy Clark, providing the goals.

The following Saturday marked Sandy's home début, in a derby draw with Hibs, when neither team could seriously trouble the goalkeepers, but his acquisition, for a mere £35,000 from Rangers, was to prove yet another master-stroke in the transfer market by MacDonald.

His first club had been Airdrie, who he joined in 1974 from Caldervale High School. He was a part-timer over eight seasons who played in over 200 league matches, scoring 89 goals for the Broomfield Club, making him the Airdrie favourite of the Seventies.

It took a £180,000 transfer to West Ham in 1982 to persuade him that full-time football was a wise choice, but in just under a

WILSON TERRIS & CO
SOLICITORS

**Monday to Friday
9am-12.30pm 2pm-5pm; Saturday 9am-12 noon**

**House Buying and Selling: Mortgage Advice:
Criminal Proceedings: Matrimonial Problems:
Debt Advice: Criminal & Industrial Injuries, etc.**

22 HILL STREET
EDINBURGH EH2 3LF; Tel: 225 1136
and
98 WESTER HAILES ROAD
(Adjacent to Wester Hailes Centre),
EDINBURGH EH14 3HR; Tel: 442 4147

MD Print & Design

SUPPLIERS TO HEART OF MIDLOTHIAN F.C.

Office:
13 Parsons Green Terrace
Edinburgh
EH8 7AG
Telephone: 031-661 6967

Workshop:
Unit 9
Castlebrae Business Centre
Peffer Place North
Edinburgh EH16 4BB
Telephone: 031-652 1184

Sandy Clark and Neil Berry – new boys

year he returned north to Rangers for £15,000 less, and then on to Hearts. Since then, of course, a coaching appointment came his way at the Club before he decided to try management at Partick Thistle, where, to use his phrase, 'the least said the better', before the striker was thrust into a caretaker/manager's role in the early part of the 1990/91 season.

The winning sequence continued with two away victories on consecutive Saturdays, when a headed goal by Jimmy Bone seven minutes from time earned the points at Dumbarton, then two from Sandy Clark, added to another Bone strike, secured a 3-2 victory over St Mirren at Love Street. Mackay, meanwhile, was still out of the first-team scheme of things through injury, but the reserve fixture against Dumbarton allowed him to make a comeback appearance, and although it would be some weeks before he could compete at first-team level, his serious injury problems for the season were a thing of the past.

The ease with which the top team had slotted into a run of positive results was ended in cruel style at Tynecastle in mid-November, when Celtic turned on a magnificent performance, featuring a Brian McClair hat-trick, to triumph 5-1. Willie

73

Johnston in the final minute gave the home fans in the 20,000 crowd some degree of consolation.

Dundee, who had won at Tynecastle in September, were to prove difficult opponents in the return fixture at Dens Park the following Saturday, and once again Hearts had to wait until the 89th minute for their goal. By that time, Lex Richardson and Robert Connor had Dundee in a winning position after little more than an hour.

Into December, and Aberdeen was the next port of call where Alex MacDonald was the scorer in a 2-1 defeat which saw Steve Cowan and Billy Stark score for the Dons and the following Saturday David Bowman would play his last match for the club.

A goal after 64 minutes by Donald Park earned Hearts a draw against Rangers and, just a few days later, they accepted an offer of £170,000 from Coventry for the midfield player. So the season which was to see Mackay, Bowman and Robertson provide a backbone for the future had seen one depart.

However, in terms of the on-going improvement in the playing staff that had to be fashioned, the offer was a good one and in any case Andy Watson had been fixed up by way of replacement for much less than half that sum, so there was scope to recruit again.

Also into midfield had come Neil Berry from Bolton Wanderers, after he had been released by the Lancashire club on condition that he join a Scottish club. He had earlier been a team-mate in England of Wayne Foster, and it was on Berry's recommendation that Hearts would later sign the striker.

Berry made his début at Tannadice and, although Hearts were beaten 5-2 – Kenny Black and Jimmy Bone scored the goals – he made a satisfactory first impression, replacing George Cowie in the second half. A second Kenny Black penalty in successive games saw Hearts defeat Morton at Tynecastle in the run-up to the New Year's Day game at Easter Road.

The match was to be a memorable one for Gary Mackay who, having fully recovered from that troublesome foot problem earlier in the season, made his 100th League appearance for the club a winning one. And he had the added satisfaction of shooting Hearts into the lead after 36 minutes, before Sandy Clark added a second 17 minutes after the interval. Hibs responded, but they needed defensive hesitance to allow Willy Jamieson to pull one back.

Then there was a five goal performance against Dumbarton in the League to keep the New Year spirit going, with Kenny Black confirming his excellent form by way of a hat-trick plus single goals from Sandy Clark and Jimmy Bone. A single goal from Gardiner Speirs at Love Street one week later was to see the beer go flat.

Eighteen days were to elapse after the weather intervened, before the Scottish Cup Third Round could be played, but it was worth waiting for, for Mackay scored four goals and Roddy McDonald and John Robertson one each, to sweep aside Inverness Caley without reply.

'Scoring in the derby was a tremendous thrill, as it always is, but the fact that it was my 100th league appearance made it doubly satisfying. After all the injury problems it was turning into a season to remember,' reflected Mackay, who celebrated his 21st birthday seven days before the four goal feat and two days after the club had defeated Morton 4-1 to win the Tennent's Sixes competition at Ingliston.

And there was an element of record-breaking in the four goals against the Highland League team, for it was the first time in 46 years that a Hearts player had scored four goals in a Scottish Cup match. That was in 1939 when Andy Black and Archie Garrett scored four each when Elgin City fared even worse than Caley, crashing out of the competition by 14 goals to one.

There were six goals at Tynecastle again five days later, in a Sunday match against Dundee, but they were evenly shared between the teams. Mackay, Robertson and young Brian McNaughton scored for the home team while John Brown, John McCormack and Graham Harvey replied for the Tayside team.

There were two away matches in the North East to come next, at Aberdeen in the League where Andy Watson scored against his old team-mates at Pittodrie, and it was left to John Robertson to score the equaliser in a 2-2 draw, one week before the little striker was to repeat the act. That was against Brechin City in the Scottish Cup where the space restrictions made Glebe Park a difficult venue, and it looked black when Bobby Torrance shot the Angus side in front with 20 minutes to go but Robertson equalised five minutes later.

The replay saw Brechin fight every bit as vigorously as they had in the first match and it took a McNaughton goal at Tynecastle to

Gary and the victorious Tennent's Sixes squad

separate the teams, and then there was a break of only three days before Rangers were faced at Tynecastle.

Andy Watson scored after only seven minutes and, although Rangers pressed with real perseverance in the early part of the second half, Hearts stayed sure for Roddy McDonald to head the second with only 10 minutes left.

Just 24 hours earlier, Jimmy Bone was appointed manager of Arbroath after playing 81 first-team games for Hearts, and scoring 16 goals in one of the shortest spells a player has had at Tynecastle whilst contributing so much.

The prelude to a Scottish Cup quarter final with Aberdeen at Tynecastle was a difficult away match against Morton, when, with European points still crucial, there were anxious glances at timepieces until Alex MacDonald came off the bench to score an 89th minute winner.

As the following Wednesday would emphasise, Hearts missed an opportunity to clinch a semi-final place despite a tremendous display against the Cup holders, and it was only justice that Sandy Clark should score the opening goal after 51 minutes.

The lead lasted until 12 minutes from time, when Eric Black's ability in the air forced an equaliser from a player who had been close to Mackay during their Scotland youth days together.

'It was a tremendous blow to hear that Eric had later given up through back trouble. He was undoubtedly one of the best Scots in the air I can remember and there is no doubt that, without the fitness problems, he would have played for his country many times,' reflected Mackay.

Black was again heavily involved in the replay at Tynecastle, but this time it was by way of an off-the-ball incident that saw Roddy McDonald ordered off after only 15 minutes, to make a difficult match considerably more taxing. Billy Stark's goal 10 minutes after the ordering off was the only one of the game.

A one-goal defeat against Dundee United at Tynecastle followed, and goals from Watson and Robertson could not cancel out replies from Johnston, McLeod and McClair at Celtic Park as a place in the UEFA Cup started to seem remote.

However, one week later goals from Sandy Clark (two), and Walter Kidd raised hopes again at Dumbarton, and at Tynecastle in the first week of April it seemed as if the recovery was continuing in the final derby game of the season.

John Robertson scored the quickest ever derby goal after 29 seconds and Hearts seemed set for a comfortable victory when Sandy Clark scored again, 20 minutes later, and there were other easy chances passed up before half time. Joe McBride was the Hibs' player who took encouragement and scored two goals in the final seven minutes.

Celtic were again painful visitors four days later, when Paul McStay and Brian McClair scored the only goals of the game, and then worse was to follow at Dens Park, when McCormack, Brown and Tosh McKinlay punished perhaps Hearts' poorest performance of the season.

There was an interesting diversion the following midweek when Hearts played Eintracht Frankfurt in a friendly when a mixture of youth and experience – with chances for Malcolm Murray and Jimmy Sandison – saw Hearts defeat the Germans 3-1. Clark, McNaughton and Robertson were the goal scorers.

Three League defeats finished the season disappointingly against Rangers, Aberdeen and St Mirren, with Brian McNaughton, an own goal, and finally Kenny Black scoring the only replies as 11 goals flew behind Henry Smith.

Into attack – Leap frog style

Recalled Mackay, 'It had been a disappointing end to a campaign which had promised so much at one point and, typically, I missed the last month through injury. . . it was that kind of season.

'But we'd seen the Hearts team of the future start to evolve and, in tasting our first sample of European football, there was tremendous incentive to take the whole thing steps forward in the coming years.' Mackay has undoubtedly been one of the most influential characters at Tynecastle through the Eighties and there could be no better tribute to 10 years of effort on his part than a Testimonial going into the Nineties.

CHAPTER SIX
Sandy Jardine
1985-86

THERE WERE far too many telephone calls to the homes of Sandy Jardine and Alex MacDonald on the Saturday morning of 3 May 1986. It was the day when Hearts were to win the championship at Dundee, if the script was to stay on course. But one by one the players telephoned to say that they were feeling off colour. On this day of all days, a virus had struck at the Tynecastle dressing-room.

Too many players - Kenny Black, Ian Jardine and Brian Whittaker, amongst others - would have to face the most taxing match of their careers a long way short of full fitness. It was even worse for Craig Levein. The central defender, who had played his part in 27 unbeaten matches in a row to set up this decision day at Dens Park, was the most badly affected. His telephone call was to pull him out of the game.

It was the worst possible start for a day when only a draw was needed to win the Championship and make Celtic's match at Love Street, where the Parkhead side still held on to hopes of a miracle, a formality. Not since 1965, when Kilmarnock snatched the league title away from Hearts at Tynecastle, were the stakes so high. And despite the horrendous late fitness problems, Dundee could not be rated in this season as the most difficult opponents.

What followed in the closing minutes of that dramatic day will never be forgotten by Hearts supporters, players and officials alike. Dundee manager, Archie Knox, had sent on midfield player Albert Kidd, a player struggling to find a regular place in the Dens Park first team, and he was to go down in history as the man who robbed Hearts of their finest hour.

Even allowing for a display that did not rank among the most fluent in their record-breaking unbeaten league run it still seemed

Karate capers from John Robertson

as if Hearts could survive. But there was an unexplained lethargy about their play, which could undoubtedly be written down to the virus, and it was during the closing 30 minutes that Sandy Jardine displayed his finest qualities.

No one ever doubted that the former Rangers player was one of the few world-class players that Scotland had produced in international terms, but it was his leadership that shone in these nerve-tingling closing moments. However, even his calm authority could not weld the Hearts defence into a unit strong enough on the day to stop Kidd scoring two late goals, thus making Celtic's five at Love Street Championship-winning goals.

It would be difficult to say where the despair was felt greatest - on the terracing or in the dressing-rooms. Hearts fans round the stadium wept as if in a state of disbelief and shock, little understanding that the scene was identical deep in the bowels of the Dens Park stand.

'Three times I tried to go in and say something that would lift them, but there was just no way,' confessed MacDonald. 'There was nothing that could be done to relieve the most hellish pain I had experienced in over 20 years in the game.'

If that defeat had been difficult to absorb, MacDonald and

Jardine had to lift the players somehow for the Scottish Cup final at Hampden Park seven days later, and not least of their problems involved picking up the legacy of that virus. Ian Jardine, Whittaker, Black and Levein had been joined by John Colquhoun, John Robertson and Neil Berry as sufferers, and the build-up to the week started with only faint hopes that Hearts would be able to field something like a recognised first team.

Aberdeen, with all their great recent Cup tradition under the guidance of Alex Ferguson, were the Cup final opponents and after the goings-on in Dundee were warm favourites to take the trophy north.

Considering what they had been through, the opening part of the match belonged to Hearts, but although they had coped well in the early period with the Aberdeen attack, they had less success in the Aberdeen penalty area. John Hewitt scored the crucial first goal, and the second, minutes after half time, and Billy Stark's third effectively ended the match as a contest.

The final result was hard on the Tynecastle team and the massive 40,000 support which travelled along the M8 to cheer them on, but there was no doubt that the legacy of the week before hung heavy on the team. It is not too fanciful to suggest that had Hearts travelled to Hampden as League Champions, with all the confidence that would have given them, then both prizes might have been destined for Edinburgh.

Although there was virtually nothing by way of consolation that seemed relevant, it was fitting that the Scottish Football Writers Association should vote Sandy Jardine their Player of the Year for that season, for his contribution in many ways had been immense. He had been a winner of the accolade before, in 1975, when both he and MacDonald were winning prizes regularly with Rangers, but, at the age of 37, his second trophy was much more satisfying.

'Winning the Player of the Year award for a second time was obviously special, but to win it with Hearts, whom I had supported since I was able to walk, was a tremendous feeling,' reflected Jardine. 'Looking back now, it still seems incredible that the players didn't get something from that season, but they should feel nothing but pride for their efforts and there will be a day when that experience, and others, will pay off.'

Jardine was later to leave Tynecastle in controversial circumstances, and for his long-time friend MacDonald, the realisation

Composed and ready – that's Sandy Jardine

that his partner had gone took a long time to completely sink in. He explained, 'Sandy was always something special, both on and off the pitch. In his later years as a player at Hearts, he was a priceless stabiliser and away from matches was constantly the source of good advice. Even in the Rangers days, when any of the younger players had problems it was always Sandy Jardine they turned to for help.

'I was surprised and very disappointed when he left Tynecastle, but life goes on . . . Hearts go on . . . and it was my place to make sure that happened.

'I kept expecting to turn a corner at Tynecastle and see Sandy walking along the corridor. He has been a close personal friend all through my career. We still talk, and I'm sure we always will. In football terms, he was unique . . . in the way that John Greig and Billy McNeill had been with the Old Firm.'

There had been little hint in the early part of the season, despite the signings of John Colquhoun from Celtic for £50,000 and Ian Jardine, that the drama reserved for May was to unfold. After all, in the opening matches of the League campaign, Hearts had drawn 1-1 with Celtic at Tynecastle, Colquhoun pointing to things to come with a 28th minute goal, but then they crashed 6-2 to St

Mirren at Love Street. There was even worse to follow on 24 August when Rangers emerged 3-1 winners at Ibrox on a day when three players were sent off by referee Douglas Hope, and the repercussions from that unsavoury afternoon were to lead to the Court of Session in Edinburgh. John Robertson had Hearts in front at the interval, but it was a fracas involving Ally McCoist, Walter Kidd and Sandy Clark that would grab the headlines on Sunday morning. The Scottish Football Association later handed out additional punishments to those contained in the disciplinary points system, but Kidd and Clark failed to convince Lord Mayfield that they were out of order. It was a strange old season indeed.

The first derby of the season, at Tynecastle one week later, briefly altered the disappointing trend that had been set in the opening three weeks when goals from Colquhoun and Clark overcame a reply from Hibs by Gordon Durie in a match where the result for Hearts was much more important than the performance and in a derby recalled by many as one of the worst ever.

The Tynecastle team then journeyed to Aberdeen with George Cowie and Paul Cherry elevated to the first team as Clark and Kidd started their 'sentences', but a re-jigged combination could not halt the Dons. Despite the fact that Hearts started the game like a whirlwind, Billy Stark headed in the opening goal in the 32nd minute, and Paul Wright and Eric Black indicated later in the match, with expert finishing, that Aberdeen on their own patch did not necessarily require to dominate the game to win comfortably.

The Premier Division season trundled on relentlessly, and Hearts went into the game against Dundee United at Tynecastle with only three points. How much these early results would mean at the end of a long, hard season could not possibly be calculated in mid-September. Nevertheless, United were contained and beaten. Roddy McDonald and John Robertson scored the goals that lifted Hearts towards the middle of the table, but still the early inconsistency had not been completely shed. Yet another away defeat was registered at Motherwell on 21 September. Ian Jardine scored his first goal for the club in the match, but Andy Harrow and John Gahagan scored one each to produce yet another bitterly disappointing game for the faithful and vociferous Hearts travelling support. There was worse to come.

Let's dance – Robbo, Roddy and Sandy

Seven days later Hearts travelled to Kilbowie Park and met Clydebank in front of only 3,500 paying customers and although injuries were once again a torment, no one could have expected that David Lloyd's solitary strike would continue a sequence that had earned Hearts only five points from eight matches.

Football has a knack of throwing up strange coincidences, and one week later, at Tynecastle, few were to realise that an undistinguished 1-1 draw was to lead directly to that final day misery at Dens Park in the following May. Especially when Derek McWilliams fired Dundee in front but Ian Jardine equalised and the record-breaking Premier Division sequence of unbeaten matches had been started, on a day when McDonald was finally able to see the end of silly goals being conceded. However, a full quarter of the league programme had gone.

Next stop was Celtic Park where Hearts would have the task of coping with unbeaten Celtic, who had in David Provan, Mo Johnston and Brian McClair that afternoon the Premier Division's most celebrated attack thus far in the season. Almost inevitably, John Robertson was the player who provided the first-half winner but it was an afternoon when the guile of Jardine and the pace of Craig Levein blunted Celtic's attack with remarkable efficiency. Perhaps of all the results that fashioned this dramatic season, that

Henry Smith, goalkeeper throughout the decade. He has missed only one competitive match since 1982 – a remarkable run of consistency

Hearts' Christmas party 1988: the players let off steam and dressed up for their annual Christmas party. How many can you recognise?

Opposite: John Colquhoun joined Hearts from Celtic in 1985, a steal at £40,000. John has matured into a player who has obtained international recognition

Above: Alan McLaren: only 19 years old and he has already played over 50 first-team games and captained the club in Europe

Opposite: Dave McPherson, a bargain buy at £350,000 from Rangers. He has developed into a full-internationalist and World Cup player

Henry Smith in action

Two horrific injuries cost Craig Levein two years out of the game. Many thought he was finished but Craig came back, not only to first-team football but to a place in the World Cup XI

Opposite: David McCreery, the little Irishman, has played over 70 times for his country, including two World Cups. A player of vast experience, his tenacious style endears him to all Hearts fans

Inset opposite: in action against Gazza

Top left: preparing for a team photograph

Bottom left: the reverse view of the photocall

*Right: John Robertson and son Mark.
Can he follow in the footsteps of his
father who has now scored over 150
competitive goals for the club?*

Celtic Park victory would be the most significant.

St Mirren, who had dealt Hearts such a humiliating defeat on the second day of the Championship programme, were soundly beaten 3-0 at Tynecastle, with Robertson scoring twice and Gary Mackay once, and the confidence being gathered within the team started to show. Aberdeen, with League Cup celebrations still ringing loud in the North, provided the next big test in Edinburgh and Hearts' new well-being was emphasised with Craig Levein's early winner. All fears of a place in the bottom half of the table were now gone and, although Hearts were still not being considered as Championship contenders, there was a new respect growing within the Scottish game.

Two consecutive draws kept the unbeaten run on course, the first at Tannadice, when Ian Jardine sent MacDonald's team in front only for Richard Gough to head an equaliser in the closing seconds. The second derby followed at Easter Road and, although there was no shortage of effort from both teams in the match, the fear of losing which had been a feature of the recent games between the teams once again rose to the surface in a no-scoring draw.

The effect that Jardine had on the Tynecastle team was to be mirrored in a tangible way the following week, when Rangers came to call. He was presented with a memento of his 1,000th senior appearance - testimony not only to his gifts but to his meticulous attention to physical detail which allowed him to compete equally with rivals sometimes half his age.

If the match was a watershed for Jardine against the team with which he enjoyed so many memorable triumphs, another former Ibrox player, Sandy Clark, felt it was time to make his mark. He scored the opening two goals in a 3-0 victory and Robertson, whose reputation as a clinical finisher had unfortunately still not been appreciated in the west of the country, snatched the third.

Seven days on, Hearts had been unbeaten in seven consecutive League matches, that aforementioned confidence was gathering strength and the goals were starting to flow. It was a combination that contained too strong a mix for Motherwell and Clydebank in the space of seven days. The Rangers result was repeated against Tommy McLean's team at Tynecastle, with Clark again scoring twice and Ian Jardine, underlining just what an immense free transfer bargain he had been, the third goal. Six goals in two

Robbo's the raider against Rangers

matches was good going by any standards, and four more were to flood past Clydebank the following week . . . with four individual scorers indicating that goals could come from any quarter in the side. Neil Berry set the tone for the afternoon with his first goal for Hearts, Clark continued his purple patch with the second, Robertson prodded in the third and Kenny Black's penalty rounded off an afternoon that went some way to wiping out that appalling defeat at Kilbowie in September.

Dens Park was to be the destination as the final month of 1985 beckoned, and, ironically, yet another crucial point was dropped to Archie Knox's workmanlike team. Kenny Black, normally so accurate from the penalty spot, was over-deliberate and saw Bobby Geddes produce a save. Only when Ian Jardine once again found the net from midfield was the Hearts' bandwagon kept in motion.

When Celtic travelled to Tynecastle for the second time, on 14 December, Hearts hadn't lost a league match since the beginning of October, and in the match previews the nation's scribes were already billing this as the match which would confirm their right to be Championship contenders. After only ten minutes, John Robertson's goal certainly seemed to justify these early predictions, but Mark McGhee's equaliser midway through the second half was a reminder that Celtic had not been convinced.

If the comprehensive defeat of Clydebank three weeks earlier

The strain game – but not for Ian Jardine against Dundee

had been sweet revenge, so too was Hearts' pre-Christmas victory at St Mirren when Kenny Black's penalty was the solitary effort to trouble referee Alistair Huett on a day when Hearts at last graced the top of the Premier Division by one point from Aberdeen.

Back to Ibrox journeyed Hearts midway between Christmas and New Year, when even Rangers' undersoil heating could not prevent Ibrox from taking on a flintlike, frosty appearance. It was no surprise that the impish John Colquhoun should find the surface to his liking, and twice skipped through the Rangers defence to earn a 2-0 victory and the second win over Rangers in this remarkable season. It's interesting to reflect that both Dave McPherson and Derek Ferguson, now such vital figures at Tynecastle, played in the losing Rangers' team that day.

Three days later, in the opening hours of 1986, Tynecastle was packed to the capacity for the visit of Hibs and a crucial test, surely, of how Hearts could cope with the pressure of not only being top of the table but having to deal with the unique demands of a New Year derby day. Ian Jardine, John Robertson and Sandy Clark were Hearts' goal heroes that chilly afternoon and, although Colin Harris replied for Hibs, the Easter Road team had been beaten comprehensively on the day in a derby clash which contained a much higher quality of football than its two predecessors.

A third game in six days beckoned Motherwell on the fourth day

Tangle time between Neil Berry and Ralph Hilne

of the year, when Fir Park was snowbound, but it was the Edinburgh players who adapted much more proficiently, even though John Reilly snatched the first goal for Motherwell before Ian Jardine, Neil Berry and John Robertson completed the best New Year Hearts fans had enjoyed for decades, with a 15th consecutive match without defeat.

By this time, the combination of Jardine at the heart of the back four and the cultured Levein had emerged as the spine of a team which was fusing the vast experience within its ranks to the exuberance of youth, with an expertise that was being bettered nowhere in the country. Levein is in no doubt that he was undergoing expert tuition. 'Sandy was a tremendous influence, not only on me but on all the players around him. So often in matches I was able to tap into his experience in difficult circumstances,' he recalled.

'It's remarkable to look back and think that, in his 38th year, he was able to do his own job and yet still watch out for others at the same time. He knew that in terms of running, he would have to do so much less. But his ability to read trouble from a distance overcame all that and there were lessons in his economy of effort that have been invaluable.'

Almost 20,000 fans saw the next act of this nine-month-long drama played out at Tynecastle against Dundee United in atrocious winter conditions. Gary Mackay gave them reward for their resilience after around an hour, but Eamon Bannon, Hearts' man before and after, equalised the tremendous long-range drive to earn Dundee United a point.

In the quest for honours in the mid-Eighties, it was a truism that the demands of playing the New Firm were just as exacting as coping with Rangers and Celtic, for the pecking order in Scottish football had been dramatically altered throughout the decade. It must then have been significant that Hearts travelled to Pittodrie on 18 January and returned with a victory that eased them four points clear of Dundee United and five ahead of Celtic, although both rivals had played fewer games. John Colquhoun was given the pleasure of earning the two points with just seven minutes remaining.

Hearts' march to the Cup final began one week later and Rangers were once again the victims at Tynecastle. Colin McAdam, signed earlier in the season on a free transfer, equalised McCoist's earlier goal, Mackay volleyed Hearts in front, and Robertson scored the winner five minutes from time, Iain Durrant having pulled Rangers level after 69 minutes of an enthralling, bruising Cup-tie in which Derek Ferguson was sent off.

Into February and Hearts moved on to Clydebank once more. They were to find Kilbowie Park a trim stadium fraught with danger, as they had early in the season. Shanks had rekindled the earlier disaster for Hearts fans after 70 minutes and, even with only ten men – Jim Given had been sent off early in the second half – Clydebank looked to be soaking up the pressure. With just four minutes left, however, Sandy Clark equalised and the statisticians could continue plotting the remarkable Hearts sequence.

Scottish football, which by now was becoming resigned to a new name adorning the Premier Division record books, held its breath for the bubble to burst. There was a moment early in the next match, when Dundee visited Gorgie, that distress signals were flying. Vince Mennie tucked the ball behind Henry Smith from six yards to send gasps round every stadium in the country. That feeling was emphasised shortly afterward when John Colquhoun dismally trundled a penalty straight to Bobby Geddes. However, the resilience contained in the players at Tynecastle soon corrected things, with Colquhoun making up for his spot-kick lapse and, in the second half, Robertson and Mackay completing a recovery that pointed them towards Celtic Park the following week and the possibility of an incredible 20th league match without a setback.

If Sandy Jardine was effervescent still in the Hearts team, Celtic had his Scotland colleague Danny McGrain still comfortably holding down a first team place at Parkhead. These were quality players, diminished not one whit by advancing years.

The match, like all Celtic-Hearts meetings, was enthralling and once again the Edinburgh players gave their opponents a start. Mo Johnston accepted with some hesitancy to place Celtic in front, but that man Robertson had equalised before half-time and everyone settled for a draw.

Amid all the speculation that was now following each Hearts league fixture was a feeling that, having despatched Rangers from the Scottish Cup, incredibly the double may be on for a team who by this time were in some way the most consistent in the country. Douglas Park, Hamilton, provided the next Cup venue and, although John Brogan scored after just a few seconds, Robertson and Mackay notched the away goals which earned a place in the Cup quarter-final six days later. The Hamilton match had been four times postponed.

In the match that pitched St Mirren in against Hearts at Tynecastle, for a place in the semi-final, Saints 'keeper, Campbell

*Quotations for all kinds of decorative works:
Private, Commercial or Industrial*

**27 HOPETOUN CRESCENT, EDINBURGH
TEL 031-556 3126/556 0020/556 1115**

That's the way to do it, says Gary Mackay

Money, fell victim to an early accident. He climbed with Sandy Clark, trying to gather a passback, and tumbled to the ground, and although he returned bravely for a short time, he gave in after John Colquhoun's opening goal and was replaced by Neil Cooper. Kenny Black and John Robertson twice took full advantage of the situation and, although Frank McGarvey scored a consolation, the tie had become one-sided long before the end.

Motherwell were Hearts' opponents on 15 March when Rangers' record of 21 consecutive Premier League games without defeat was matched. Against the progressive Lanarkshire team, however, the game was anything but a foregone conclusion, though the Tynecastle players coped well with their early flourish and responded with first-half goals from Roddy McDonald and John Robertson to strengthen Hearts' grip at the top of the league table.

It was at Easter Road that the task of establishing the new record would be undertaken and Hibs, without a victory in two attempts, were predictably difficult opponents. Sandy Clark, as he had done so often before in the campaign, earned reward for his persistence before half time, but Steve Cowan's header soon after the interval gave the home fans the encouragement they craved. Just a couple of minutes later, however, a Robertson header was handled on the line and the striker took the penalty himself to register a seventh point from their city rivals that season.

Just three days later, St Mirren were the next victims, this time at Tynecastle when they fell by three goals to nil. Campbell Money, who had been such an unfortunate injury victim in the previous meeting between the teams, worked tirelessly to prevent Hearts from building on John Robertson's interval lead, but even he admitted defeat late in the match when an impudent back-heel from Robertson beat him again, and Sandy Clark finished the contest in the final minute.

Still there was no halting this team on a relentless march toward prizes, as Rangers were to find out in Edinburgh the following Saturday. This time, Nicky Walker and Hugh Burns lined up alongside McPherson in a Rangers side but this permutation fared no better than the last. Robertson cleverly lofted the ball over Walker's head for the first and added a second from the penalty spot just after half-time. And, although Ally McCoist converted a penalty to bring Rangers back, briefly, into the game, Sandy Clark, as he had done against St Mirren in the previous match, celebrated a last-minute goal.

The first indication of the real nitty-gritty presented itself at Hampden Park on 5 April, when Dundee United were to be faced in the Scottish Cup semi-final. In all matches, Hearts had played 28 games without defeat before going to the national stadium and, although United had regularly fared badly there, it was only against the teams from the west that they traditionally struggled on the big occasion. They travelled confidently.

The pattern of the match was established early on, with Hearts using their three front players willingly, and United, just a little cautiously, trying to establish their grip on the game. However, the Hearts plan worked better when Colquhoun scored the goal that would earn an appearance in the final, after only 13 minutes. Maurice Malpas and Dave Narey both tried to deny him space as the tiny striker spied a volley, but they were a fraction late as his spectacular shot sped high into the net. United had a chance to make amends just one week later when the teams met at Tannadice in the League, but if they escaped with a single goal defeat in the Cup, they were to fare much worse in, arguably, Hearts' best performance of the season. A left-foot drive from Robertson midway through the opening half set the tone for an exhilarating afternoon for the thousands of Hearts fans who thronged Tayside. Henry Smith had to produce heroics from Malpas after the interval before Colquhoun, of all people, made a telling header in the United penalty area to feed Sandy Clark for the second. Robertson and Colquhoun combined for a third stunning goal after 66 minutes and it was Robertson who skipped round Billy Thomson for the finish, in front of the adoring Hearts fans.

Three league matches to go and a Cup final, and as Hearts were asked to produce that one final trick, the pressure was heightened when a live television audience watched the league match against Aberdeen at Tynecastle on 20 April. For once, nervousness appeared to attack the home players and while they struggled to capture composure, Aberdeen's experience earned them the ascendancy... and John McMaster's opening goal with 18 minutes left. Ironically that setback, from a hotly disputed penalty, seemed to banish the edginess from the Hearts play and for the first time in the game they placed Aberdeen under pressure. It seemed that the Dons would never crack, but they did with just three minutes remaining. Sandy Jardine, still the one unflustered player on view, tempted the Aberdeen back four with a lofted clearance into the penalty area, and when Robertson got the first hesitant touch, Colquhoun finished the move off.

Hearts' last home game of the season saw Clydebank as visitors, and there was relief, if not satisfaction, with the 1-0 victory. Gary Mackay scored the decisive goal and despite Celtic's late push that kept them in contention for the final day, Mackay's goal seemed to be the one that would win the Championship. Then it was on to Dens Park and the start of seven heartbreaking days.

The Skol Cup during the early part of the season had not been so exhilarating, and ironically that campaign was to end in the same way that the Scottish Cup effort finished, at the hands of Aberdeen. Walter Kidd, John Colquhoun and John Robertson scored goals that eased them past Montrose in round two, while Brian McNaughton and Paul Cherry were the youngsters on target against Stirling Albion in the next stage. Pittodrie had 15,000 spectators engrossed for the fourth round, but it was the home fans who went home happy. It was no consolation for the Tynecastle team that Roddy McDonald's clearance struck Eric Black just a few yards from goal, and the ball rebounded past Henry Smith.

So a season that might have earned Sandy Jardine a most marvellous climax to a career produced nothing tangible. But he himself was able to cast a professional eye back over the experience, once the initial disappointment had worn off.

'The despair that was felt during the final week of the season will never completely go away. In the years ahead, it will still crop up in football conversations in every corner of the country,' he said. 'Although we just needed a break or two at particular times to make sure, it should be remembered that the team were going through a development which was taking them through a complete division in Scottish football. On the way, the players re-wrote Scottish football records and despite the disappointment were better men for it.'

In the years ahead, it was to become clear that their experience had in no way diminished the hunger for success.

CHAPTER SEVEN

Craig Levein
1986-87

TWO TINY staples have carried Craig Levein through the most remarkable recovery of the Eighties and ultimately to the World Cup in Italy. Two tiny metal fixings hold together a ligament, snapped and shortened, and a career that has been miraculously saved.

It was Alex MacDonald who first coined the phrase, 'the Craig Levein story is a fairytale.' It has often been repeated in many quarters, but does not lose any of its significance by being uttered again and again. However, the fairytale did not require a magic wand to provide the happy ending. It was the sharp cutting edge of the scalpel and the dedicated skills of a Glasgow surgeon that saw the tall, athletic Fifer have the chance to bring his mental steel into the equation.

The torture for Levein started during a reserve match against Hibs at Easter Road, when astonishingly there was no tackle involved in the incident that was to see him helped out of the Hibs ground, unable to put any weight on the stricken right leg.

The problem was not difficult to diagnose but in medical circles there were differing opinions on how best the injury should be treated. The first view taken was that of Mr Malcolm McNicol, an Edinburgh surgeon with a great wealth of experience in dealing with sports injuries. His counsel was that rest over a long period of time would allow the damaged ligament to knit together, with the strength that's required to stand up to the rigours that the legs of the professional footballer must resist. That required the central defender to accept the role of a reluctant spectator from the Thursday evening of 16 October until his return to action in Inverness, during a testimonial match against Caley, almost a full year later, on the second last day of September.

It was a crushing blow to lose a player, who was not only starting

95

to catch the international eye but who could have been traded to Tottenham or Rangers for vast amounts of money, for such a long period. That, though, was not the main concern for MacDonald and Jardine. They could organise the cover that would keep Hearts close on the heels of the Premier Division's hierarchy. The priority was for Craig to recover fully and get back into a first-team jersey in the same impressive shape as before.

However there were other problems to consider outside the main medical worry over whether or not the injury would heal. There was the mental anguish and inevitable doubt that would invade a young mind and the fact that his general fitness level would drop alarmingly during the period of recuperation.

'The muscle wastage that occurred during the long period away from day to day work had to be seen to believed. There was absolutely no strength in the leg at all when the time came to start the slow process of catching full fitness,' recalled Levein. 'As far as the mental part of it was concerned, I can honestly say that I always felt deep down that I would play again, at the very highest level. There were times of doubt, sure, but the bottom line was a belief that I would be back. After the injury was ready to take some work, there were endless hours in the gym, building up the muscles round the knee, for they would be the pillars that would take the strain when the ligament was put to the test.'

That test first came in that match up north and again the following Saturday against Rangers. A fairly uneventful 0-0 draw at Tynecastle later in that season - on 16 January, 1988 in fact - came to be tragic and symbolic. For it was in that match, just in front of the North Stand, that the sight of Craig Levein, once again spread prostrate as he tried to make a clearance from the right full-back position, was to send a cold shiver down the spine of everyone at Tynecastle.

Days later the ligament trouble was confirmed again and a more radical solution was mooted by Peter Scott, a Glasgow surgeon who specialised in surgery of this nature. The ligament would be severed, made good again and recovery would be complete. That was the theory and in Mr Scott, Craig was to discover a man who not only had the dexterity to deal with the surgical problem, but someone who had such faith in the operation that Levein's mental capacity to cope with a second serious setback was significantly enhanced.

In simple terms, the operation involved a piece of tendon being

Back at work – Craig Levein

placed between the ends of the ligament and reinforced with polypropylene. It was then stretched until the tension was right, and the two staples that bear so much responsibility were clipped in place.

The results of that operation are now a matter of record. It would not be until January 1989 that the name Levein would once again appear in the Hearts first team, against Dundee United at Tannadice. Once again he returned to action in a no-scoring draw and remarkably, after so much trauma, his comeback appearance saw the Sunday newspapers almost without exception vote him the man of the match.

There was also the great sight and sound of both sets of supporters giving him a warm and noisy reception as he took his first, nervous steps on to the pitch, after surviving a period of two years and three months that few players could have come through.

All that seemed a million miles away when, as a 19 year-old, he was the subject of a change of direction in Hearts' recruitment policy after Alex MacDonald and Sandy Jardine needed very little by way of evidence that Levein should become a Hearts player. In the opening half of the Eighties there had been no chance for the club to indulge in the luxury of buying players for the future. That was a luxury that belonged to the Liverpools, Manchester Uniteds and Rangers of this football world, and not to a club who had spent years perfecting the art of survival. But now the Tynecastle management would change. Levein would be a signing for the future even if, with their stretched resources, the men who sanctioned the signing of the £30,000 cheque would need to play him at Ibrox within days of the ink drying.

It was indicative of the player's potential that, after only 60 matches in Division Two and less then one week's full-time training, he would acquit himself well on that October afternoon against Rangers, when two goals from Sandy Clark and one from John McDonald made Levein's performance a welcome consolation.

'Craig was quality, it was simple as that,' said Jardine at the time. 'We knew that there were many other clubs watching him, but that was not the only reason we acted quickly to take him to Tynecastle.

'We both agreed that Craig had everything a young player needed to make it in the game. He was quick, was very powerfully built for a teenager and had good touch coupled with accuracy of distribution. The combination is very rarely seen in the lower divisions.'

Levein's introduction to the Hearts first team would display the quality that struck the men who had such faith in his future. With Sandy and Roddy McDonald established as the central defensive pairing, his pace and power were used in a wide position on the right. For a big man, operating at a new, higher level, he looked perfectly at home.

Such a rapid introduction to the first team in that début season meant that the Scotland Youth cap, who had played his football at junior level with Lochore Welfare, would make 25 first-team appearances - the club would finish fifth-top - and Europe would beckon once again.

Europe was also on the agenda in season 1986/87 a season which would serve as such a vivid reminder to everyone - through Levein's misfortunes - that in football, despair and joy can be one fraction of a second away. However, the campaign started in a far more glamorous and more unlikely setting.

The holiday and income-tax haven of the Isle of Man had developed a pre-season competition as part of their publicity machine and, as part of their preparation programme, Hearts were to meet Stoke City, Wigan Athletic and Bohemians from Ireland in the Football Festival. There were no goals in the opening game against Stoke - not for Hearts anyway - but the Midlands club did score once, to start the competition off on a low note. The honour of collecting Hearts' first goal that season fell to John Colquhoun against Wigan in a 1-1 draw. The tiny winger with the big heart had been yet another inspired bit of transfer business by Alex MacDonald the previous summer. David Hay had been unable to include him in the Celtic first team regularly, so £50,000 was sufficient to coax him to Tynecastle. Right through the record-breaking unbeaten run he had been ever present, but if he had been impressive with his darting runs to the line and accurate final ball into the box, this season would add a lethal touch to his armoury.

That goal against the team from Lancashire in the Isle of Man was the first of 19 he would claim during the season, an incredible total for a player who, although comfortable raiding through the middle, was nevertheless regarded as an out-and-out wide man.

The Hearts squad 1986/87

Now the highly respected chairman of the PFA in Scotland, Colquhoun brought not only his skills to Hearts in that Celtic deal, but also an authoritative and credible voice on all football matters as they affect players.

Over the years Levein and Colquhoun have developed a close friendship with one another and, like the rest of the staff at Hearts, the winger who had the then Stirling Albion manager Alex Smith to thank for his introduction to professional football, would be a great ally during the injury-ridden period that was about to start for Levein.

'Players with genuine width and pace are so hard to find and John gave our play a vital option from the day he made his début in a pre-season trip to West Germany the previous summer,' recalled Levein. 'When the wee man is on song, the only option for a defender is to let him past or foul him, and for the back players he is always ready to come deeper to the halfway line and make himself available for a pass.'

The trend started by Colquhoun that evening against Wigan continued in the next game against Bohemians which Hearts won 3-1 - Andy Watson and the on-trial Willie Irvine scored the others - and then Watford came to Edinburgh to complete the warm-up programme. The English First Division side had made their way to Scotland from a series of games in Sweden and so, unlike many teams from south of the border at this time of the year, were well enough forward to give Hearts the ideal competitive 90 minutes before the season started in earnest.

So well had the players summered under MacDonald and Jardine - that period had included a three-match trip to the West Indies on the back of the League and Cup disappointments the previous May - that there was zest and no lingering despondency about their play. Colquhoun and Sandy Clark scored the Hearts counters in a 2-1 win that was the ideal preamble for a season in which the players would have to try and achieve a target that would prove impossible – to better second-top in the Championship.

The opening league match of the season meant a journey to Love Street, and if one point was a trifle disappointing, the fact that no goals were conceded gave the side a solid, if unspectacular, start to the long haul ahead.

Hamilton Accies and the newly-promoted Falkirk were visitors to Tynecastle within four days in mid-August. John Robertson's first of the season was enough to see off the Lanarkshire team while Andy Watson followed up his pre-season goal with the winner against Falkirk.

The following midweek saw a black night for the club when Montrose travelled from Angus in the Skol Cup and, despite having 95 per cent of the pressure, the goal to settle the players would not arrive - but two on the break at the other end did - and the first knockout competition of the season was over at the first time of asking.

Up at Tannadice the following Saturday, something similar awaited, with United winning 1-0 on a day when Hearts fans saw the forward play of Wayne Foster, signed on a free transfer from Preston North End, for the first time. All that was forgotten the following week, however, when goals from Ian Jardine, Sandy Clark and John Robertson earned an emphatic 3-1 win against Hibs at Easter Road, when Clark's power in the air was a factor that Hibs could not cope with, and Sandy Jardine's performance in defence, despite having a bad foot gash, kept the back door firmly closed. With Dukla Pargue to be faced in the UEFA Cup later in the month, there was a welcome chance to face new opposition when Manchester United were visitors to Tynecastle for a friendly on 2 September. Andy Watson and Ian Jardine counted in a 2-2 draw, watched by almost 12,000 fans.

Clydebank featured as the next home opponents in the league and as always gave Hearts an anxious time, but a first goal of the season from Gary Mackay and Foster's opener for the club secured the two points that overall supremacy deserved.

Ever-present Levein was outstanding in the next fixture when, up at Aberdeen, Hearts were 1-0 winners thanks to a Sandy Clark goal. That surely would send everyone into the midweek European match with great optimism ... but the team from Czechoslovakia boasted a marvellous pedigree.

Although they travelled to Tynecastle having taken only one point from their opening three games, Dukla had been third in the Championship last season and had reached the semi-final of the Cup Winners' Cup. Alex MacDonald's warning that Hearts were tangling with one of Europe's top clubs was justified. Their skipper, Jan Fiala, was perhaps their most accomplished current player, with 50 caps for the Czech national side, but Stanislav Griga was his country's top scorer the previous term with 16 goals, so there was quality at the other end of their team as well.

All that was forgotten in the opening minute of the match, watched by an attendance of 18,869, for a left-foot drive from Wayne Foster, after Sandy Clark had nudged on an Ian Jardine throw-in, gave the watching legions a start they could only have dreamed of. But the experience contained in the Prague team's line-up soon became a factor and a close-in equaliser from Tomas Fitzl had the teams level. And there was worse to follow ... when Josef Kluckly drove Dukla ahead from a Peter Rada pass after 63 minutes.

Despite the fact that Hearts were giving away years of maturity in terms of European wisdom, the players buckled down in the closing 30 minutes and, assisted by the deafening encouragement from the crowd, pulled off a tremendous victory. Crucially, Sandy Clark levelled things three minutes later before the Czechs had time to settle on their lead, forcing goalkeeper Peter Kostelnik into an error under pressure, and he seemed unhappy again, 12 minutes from time, when John Robertson nipped in a close-in winner after the keeper had failed to hold a Foster shot.

A lead had been established for the visit to Prague two weeks later, but the two away goals which the army side had snatched had given Hearts a big task behind the Iron Curtain. A single-goal win would take Dukla through, providing they did not concede any more than two goals themselves.

There were intervening things for Hearts to attend to, however, the first of which was a home Premier Division match against Motherwell. The European exertions of midweek had not taken too much out of the players and a crushing 4-0 win was evidence of that, courtesy of goals from John Robertson, John Colquhoun, Andy Watson and Sandy Clark.

An away point at Dens Park kept confidence high for the journey to Prague in midweek and, with the squad travelling by scheduled flights on the Tuesday, via London, there was the chance for the experienced and wily Czechs to indulge in some subtle gamesmanship. As they approached Prague airport - the wheels of the aircraft had already been released - there was a surprise surge of power and a thrust back up to around 6,000 feet, where they started to circle the runway in that frustrating way a shuttle journey to busy Heathrow is often elongated. The pilot indeed confirmed by tannoy that there would be a delay, owing to the busy early-evening traffic using the country's major airport. The problem was, from the air they couldn't see any aircraft.

After some 40 minutes they did land quietly enough, to the usual sarcastic cheers, and had that airborne suspicion confirmed. Not only was the place a picture of peace in the skies, but there wasn't a single plane to be seen on the tarmac. The game had started, 24 hours ahead of kick-off.

That relatively short delay was just a taste of things to come, however, as grim-faced soldiers supervised the never-ending visa and customs formalities, as the players, already weary from the journey, stood in line at just one passport check-point in an otherwise deserted and tranquil terminal building. The result of all this was an obvious, if reluctant, decision by Alex MacDonald that food and rest would be the priorities for the players, and the chance to have a loosening-up training session was lost.

The match in the Juliska Stadium was as tight-fought as the first leg had been, and with only 3,500 paying to see the tie, depending on where you sat the venue could have been anywhere. Our position, high in the modern, sweeping stand allowed us to look over toward the club building and changing rooms, which resembled the facilities that a down-market junior club would provide. Viewing from there into the stand, over the dry, somewhat uneven surface did, however, reaffirm that Hearts were in a venue befitting a European tie of this standard. Away to the left stood the grey, austere army barracks that betrayed the links Dukla historically have with the armed forces, to complete a strange setting.

The opening 45 minutes gave little by way of clues as to who was the home side. It was Hearts who exerted control and, on two occasions in particular, the hundreds who had travelled so far to encourage the team almost enjoyed reward for the loyalty - John Colquhoun and Wayne Foster almost shooting goals that would have ended the contest.

Into the second half, Dukla at last found their flow and, after a period of unrelenting pressure, that expert chance-taker Griga sent a right-foot drive from 12 yards past Henry Smith . . . but the match was still not over.

John Robertson was tumbled in the box for what seemed a certain penalty and then Andy Watson, who had replaced Walter Kidd, tucked in a close-in half-chance only to see the linesman's flag rescue the home players, who were clearly unsettled and nervous of Hearts' willingness to attack.

That tiny break, which is so often denied away teams in the three European club competitions, would not fall the way of the men in maroon though, and it was back to bread and butter, although in a highly-charged atmosphere, against Rangers at Tynecastle. There was no hint of weariness in the home team's start to the game and, after Neil Berry had neatly stroked in Kenny Black's corner in the 17th minute, there were further chances for Black, John Robertson and Sandy Clark to tie the points up. None were accepted though and Hearts were to regret this four minutes after the interval, when Davie Cooper took on and drifted through four challenges, before beating Henry Smith from close in.

There was a 2-0 defeat at Celtic the following week, and another no-scoring meeting with St Mirren . . . and that was the last first-team match Craig Levein would play that season, as the fateful reserve fixture at Easter Road loomed the following midweek. However, Roddy McDonald resumed his partnership with Sandy Jardine as the season rolled on relentlessly without the stricken defender, and there was no panic in the ranks at Douglas Park when Gary Mackay, John Colquhoun and Wayne Foster goals ensured both points in a 3-1 win. Colquhoun and Mackay were the marksmen again against Dundee United at Tynecastle in a 2-2 draw, followed by a disappointing 2-0 defeat at Falkirk which brought on the second derby of the season, watched by 22,178 fans

Dave McPherson in Rangers colours at Tynecastle

at Tynecastle.

Hibs took the lead after 18 minutes when Joe McBride floated a free-kick in off the post, but then Hearts took control and Gary Mackay shot the equaliser from the penalty spot following a handling offence by Callum Milne. Then, two goals from John Colquhoun and one from Roddy McDonald as Hearts were 3-0 winners at Clydebank were followed by Colquhoun and Robertson finishes in a fine 2-1 victory over Aberdeen at home, and two more victories were to extend the winning November sequence to four. Roddy McDonald scored twice at Fir Park and Neil Berry scored the third in a 3-2 win and, seven days later at home against Dundee, Colquhoun, Black and Robertson were the men who mattered in a 3-1 success.

However, there were mixed fortunes against the Old Firm going into December, with a single Neil Berry goal against Celtic in a home match in some way making up for a 3-0 defeat at Ibrox the previous week. Two hundred and seventy minutes without a goal were registered in games between St Mirren and Hearts at Love Street the following Saturday, but there was no shortage of goals seven days later when Hamilton keeper Rikki Ferguson was beaten seven times. John Robertson led the way with two, and

On target – John Colquhoun against Dundee

there was proof that goals could come from all over the Hearts side with Sandy Jardine, Roddy McDonald, Gary Mackay, John Colquhoun and Sandy Clark weighing in with one each.

The two goals from Robbo started a four-game sequence that would confirm his place as the club's top scorer . . . he grabbed one in the 3-1 defeat at Tannadice and two and one respectively in comfortable wins against Falkirk and Clydebank. There were four goals, equally shared in the 6 January derby at Easter Road where John slammed in the double and, after a barren week down to the January cold snap, Andy Watson put one past his old mates at Aberdeen which unfortunately couldn't avert a 2-1 defeat.

Gary Mackay, also scoring freely, hit the winner at Dens Park before an incredible Scottish Cup marathon started against Kilmarnock, which needed three attempts at a settlement. There were no goals at Tynecastle in the first of the trio and, in the Rugby Park re-match Wayne Foster had to cancel out a Bryson strike for Killie, and not even a period of extra time could separate the two teams. A second replay - again in Ayrshire - did have the desired effect, though, and it was Hearts who took control. Gary Mackay steered in the opening goal from 15 yards and, after Kenny Black had neatly nodded in the second, a last-minute Wayne Foster effort made Paul Martin's home goal seem pointless.

A home tie against Celtic was the reward for persistence against the Ayrshire team, but the three matches had taken a physical toll and, with Sandy Jardine out of the side with a calf injury, fresh legs were hard to come by. A 5-2 defeat by Rangers at home, when John Robertson scored twice from the penalty spot, highlighted the weariness, but recovery was on hand against Celtic in the Championship when a Wayne Foster goal won a point in Glasgow ... and then the Cup battle in Edinburgh was on.

Typically, the game was one of the features of the season, with the woodwork saving both sides in the opening half. Alan McInally rattled the Hearts' bar in the 18th minute and then a Roddy McDonald header thumped Pat Bonner's right-hand post. Anton Rogan headed a Kenny Black cross against his own cross bar in the second half, but John Robertson's free-kick ten minutes from time eventually earned a quarter-final place. Awarded against Roy Aitken for a foul on Walter Kidd, Robbo struck the free-kick from 22 yards with tremendous power and the ball took a deflection as it swept past Bonner. A home tie against Motherwell was next.

A place in Europe was still possible from a League position and that was assisted by an away draw at Fir Park where Robertson was the man with the finish, and it was Colquhoun who claimed the headlines against St Mirren seven days later in a 1-0 win. The two scorers were reversed in the next two weeks, with Colquhoun earning a 1-0 victory against Hamilton at Douglas Park and J. R. the scorer in a 1-1 draw with Motherwell in the Scottish Cup. That meant a hazardous replay in Lanarkshire in midweek, and the tie lived up to that difficult appearance with no goals going into the final five minutes. That was when a Kenny Black shot thumped off the woodwork and Colquhoun darted in to flash a close-in header past John Gardiner. St Mirren and a Hampden date would be next in the Cup.

There were two reasons why Hearts wanted to dismiss the Paisley team from the competition. First, the obvious one, to reach the final and go for the trophy that Tynecastle fans craved so dearly. In addition, however, a St Mirren win in the Cup would almost certainly cost Hearts a place in the UEFA Cup next season, with fifth place looking good, but not good enough. Two draws against Falkirk and Clydebank had done no great harm to the Championship table placing, nor had a 2-1 home derby win against Hibs, to stay unbeaten by their city rivals that season. Roddy McDonald and Sandy Clark had kept the sequence going. Both players were back in action in the semi-final the following Saturday, but that turned out to be a big let-down. Suspensions

'Which way?' asks David Kirkwood

and injuries badly limited team selection - on top of Levein being absent, Kidd, Whittaker and Robertson were all missing and things looked bleak when Ian Ferguson scored for St Mirren in 31 minutes.

The Paisley team, who were to go on and defeat Dundee United in the final, were proving difficult to overcome but Gary Mackay gave Hearts the lift they needed with a skilfully struck shot from a George Cowie pass with 16 minutes left in which to win the match. It was Alex Smith's side that struck the decisive goal late in the game, however, Frank McGarvey turning on a Kenny McDowell pass to drive low past Henry Smith, with a replay only six minutes away.

Europe, for a second successive season, depended on Dundee United defeating Saints and, although form held up well in the closing weeks, the six points gained from victories over Motherwell and Celtic and draws with Dundee United and Aberdeen retained a top-five place, with the restriction that only domestic football would be available in the coming season.

So it was very much a case of what might have been, and that was not better reflected than in the months of frustration endured by Craig Levein. Together with his own personal anguish, he was also obliged to watch his team-mates set up so much by way of reward for another season of unstinting graft, and watch it all evaporate in that semi-final defeat against St Mirren. This inability to contribute was something that he would have to get used to over the next 18 months, but a deep strength of character has shone through Levein's darkest days, not only to take him through a career crisis, but to make him a stronger individual in his life thereafter. He required assistance, inevitably, and he is lavish in his praise of the club who stood by him so loyally during a time when there were so many gloomy forecasts about his ability to fulfil the potential spotted at Central Park in 1984. So much so that he has committed himself to the club for an extended period, when a move would still have been a distinct possibility. 'The club were good to me, so I felt it was only right that I should repay some of that loyalty,' he explained. The fact that Dave McPherson had also been persuaded to stay on at Tynecastle was another plus factor, proving once again that retaining top talent at a club has a knock-on effect. Players want to stay where the good players congregate.

All together now – Craig and Mo Johnston

The two people who provided the biggest crutch for Craig during the darker hours, though, live their daily lives half an hour from Tynecastle Park. His wife, Carol, gave him the support and encouragement he needed away from football, and the birth of daughter Christie during the second period of recovery was a most timely arrival. That's life all over, Craig . . . the ladies always get the last word.

110

CHAPTER EIGHT

John Robertson
1987-88

GOALS HAVE been John Robertson's business since the first time he pulled on a football strip. There have been many attempts to change his game over the years and, although he has worked tirelessly on other aspects of his repertoire, he remains essentially a finisher. Tampering with the natural instincts of a man with such an individual and priceless gift is a very dangerous game indeed. He scores by instinct, by radar almost, and over the decade his trick has proved infallible.

In his first full season in the Hearts team his haul was 22 goals, including three hat-tricks, and in the eight months before his transfer to Newcastle, he had celebrated his best-ever performance, scoring 31 times. At the start of season 1990/91, the 25-year-old had 177 goals to his credit so it will not be too many months before he passes the double century, a remarkable achievement for a player whose career has been spent with a team that has needed to chase rivals rather than lead them.

But simple statistics do not tell the whole story. There have been many players over the years who have, in numerical terms, been prolific goalscorers, but it is important to assess the performance against the quality of opposition. For Robertson has scored consistently against the best teams in the land. This, as much as the total involved, is the mark of his ability. The best international defenders, from many different countries, have failed to curb his talent.

It was therefore no surprise that John should score when making a belated Scotland début in the European Championship match against Romania, and that important first-half goal was typically Robertson.

'It sums up everything that you need to know about John,' reflected his former Salveson's Boys Club team-mate Gary

Mackay. 'So many players would have tried to swing at the ball as it dropped, six yards out. The danger there would have been getting under it, and the shot going high over. His speed of thought in taking the ball on the half-volley with the sole of the boot was just what I would expect. The finish wasn't glamorous, but so effective.'

The story has been the same from his school-days at Parson's Green and Portobello, through the Scotland Schools' team, youth football and then Hearts. But if the striker's ability in the penalty area is to a large degree in-born and self-taught, he is quick to point out that several players through his time at Tynecastle – and briefly at Newcastle – have had a distinct influence on his game.

In common with so many others at the club, when asked to recall the Eighties, there are two names that crop up constantly. Jimmy Bone and Willie Johnston are never far away from any Hearts conversation, and Robertson still taps into their experience to this day. 'So much of what Jimmy told me years ago has happened just the way he said it would. Between the two of them, they had such a wealth of knowledge and it was a lucky day for the younger players at the club when they brought that to Tynecastle,' praised John. 'Not only did they have the tricks of the trade, they had a great way of passing everything on. It's no surprise to see Jimmy doing so well as a manager – he has all the gifts needed to do well in that job.

'Looking back, it's very difficult to describe the impact they had on Hearts. I shudder to think where we would have gone without them because they filled a gap in the staff at the time that was crucial.

'We had all the young players, and the older brigade, but no one in between. Jimmy and Willie filled that void and were responsible for the creation of the great atmosphere there was around the place.

'Alex MacDonald and Sandy Jardine knew, of course, that they would do that and I'm sure there were many little things that went on which they left Jimmy and Willie to sort out, rather than try to do it with a heavy hand.'

Being a front player, it was inevitable that Bone would be his mentor, and Robertson also jealously guards the lessons passed on by Sandy Clark while the two players struck up a playing partnership in the later years of the decade just ended.

Concentration is the name of Sandy Clark's game

'Sandy was a completely different type of player, but he too had points to make that were important to me. Jimmy was in many ways an out-of-the-box player who liked to play passes into the box, while the trick with Sandy was to be in the right place to connect with the little flicks and breaks that came off his physical presence in the penalty area,' he went on.

It is clear from all this that the five-foot six-inch striker has one great ability to go with his many professional assets . . . he likes to listen. As a developing player, that turned out to be a handy attribute with Bone around.

'He would bawl, shout, curse, prod, encourage and con me. And all that would be in one game, depending on what the circumstances were and the frame of mind I was in at the time,' remembered Robertson. 'Our game is all about confidence. If the goals are going in, everything is great, but if they're not then the head can go down a bit and you start doubting the things that have worked so well in the past.

'Jimmy told me once you don't always have to be scoring – that there will be spells when they just won't go in – and that's when you have to rely on the other players doing their bit. "When the goals dry up, just keep running and chasing, keeping the defenders busy, and let someone else take the responsibility for the goals," he would say.

'That was an important lesson, because when a spell like that does come along I can now take the pressure off myself and do it the Bone way until the goals start to flow again, which thankfully they always have after a lean period.'

So, it was armed with all that wisdom that Robertson and his mates tackled the 1987/88 season, with a return to the European arena the top priority and, after that, any big prize that might end the club's search for a trophy. The pre-season period took the team to West Germany, with mixed results against five teams in eight days, but final scorelines were not important as the conditioning for a hard season in the Premier Division was sought after, and there was a chance for new signings Dave McPherson and Hugh Burns to get to know everyone.

It was the first home match that season, against Newcastle on 3 August, that would put the finishing touches to the planning stages, but also, as John Robertson would discover later, make a massive impact on his career. The game gave Newcastle manager Willie McFaul a first-hand chance to watch him in action.

The match was won by the team from the north-east and, although there wasn't a Robbo goal to record from the game, his mobility and general menace in the penalty area clearly lingered in the Irishman's mind. He had seen the striker he wanted at St James' Park. Robertson had scored two goals in the West Germany sequence of matches and that was matched in the first competitive game of the season, against Falkirk at Tynecastle, when the 4-2 victory saw John Colquhoun and Sandy Clark with a goal each.

Colquhoun had been at his impish best in the match and although goals from the giants – Stuart Burgess and Crawford Baptie – put a slight damper on the day, there was enough evidence to suggest that the players were in good shape and that the trip to meet Celtic the following week could be fruitful.

And it should have been too, for the team were comfortably holding the Glasgow side with only four minutes left when Dave McPherson looked to be fouled in the box prior to Mark McGhee shooting the only goal of the match.

Having two good penalty claims turned down did not help the mood and, although a Robertson penalty against St Mirren seven days later earned a point in a 1-1 draw, the Celtic defeat would be

Spot the ball. John Robertson, Graham Roberts and Jimmy Nichol

an irritant for some weeks.

But the Skol Cup brought consolation the following midweek when Kilmarnock were on the end of a 6-1 drubbing at Tynecastle. This was one of the games when Robbo would rely on others, with the goals being supplied by Neil Berry, Dave McPherson, Gary Mackay, Wayne Foster and two from Sandy Clark.

Clark hit two on the next Saturday when Dundee United were beaten 4-1, a rare heavy defeat for Jim McLean's team, with Ian Jardine and Robertson goals from the penalty spot completing a very satisfying scoreline. Then Clyde were next to feel the Hearts backlash.

The Tynecastle game was to decide who would go through to the quarter-final of the Skol Cup and it was Robertson who supplied the vital touches, the first a swift close-in header in the opening half, and the second a penalty with seven minutes left.

The opening derby of the season came next on a busy schedule when Alan Rough had one of those days. He defied Hearts for long spells but, when victory arrived for the home team, it was Roughie who would be given most of the blame. The Scotland 'keeper

It's hand's off for Hans Segers

misjudged a pass from Walter Kidd into the box and, when John Colquhoun made the vital touch to nick the ball past the 'keeper, his cutback was fired high into the net by the man himself . . . Robertson.

There was a goal by the country's top scorer at Ibrox in the next round of the Skol Cup on 2 September, but that was scant

A striking deal – between John Robertson and Wayne Foster

consolation on an evening when the roof fell in. Ian Durrant and Ally McCoist scored twice each as the quest for a cup seemed as far away as ever. Their League form continued to be solid and sure, however, and two points were gleaned from the trip to Cappielow, with Colquhoun and Robertson scoring one each in a 2-1 victory, and three more straight wins followed in the Championship programme.

Motherwell called at Tynecastle next and were beaten by a single Allan Moore goal - Colquhoun grabbed two and Robertson one at Dens Park - and, in another away victory at Dunfermline, Colquhoun again displayed his well-being.

After a 4-3 victory in the Highlands against Inverness Caledonian, Hearts and Rangers played out a no-scoring draw at Tynecastle, but the victories rolled again soon, with impressive wins against Aberdeen and Falkirk inside four days. The Dons lost 2-1 at Tynecastle despite leading from an early Jim Bett penalty, for Robertson and then Dave McPherson responded within three minutes of each other to win both points, and at Brockville there was clear evidence that the fitness level of the players was exemplary. Coming off a two-games-a-week programme, Colquhoun twice, Wayne Foster, Robertson and Ian Jardine

117

struck with no mercy as Falkirk could only muster a Rab Stewart reply in what was a devastating display.

There was a derby defeat to bring everyone back down to earth at Easter Road in mid-October, however, and although Robbo continued a remarkable scoring record against the Capital rivals, Eddie May and Paul Kane both scored to swing the verdict Hibs' way. Twenty-four hours later Walter Kidd had his marvellous service to the club rewarded when Everton very generously provided testimonial opposition without charge. The torrential rain that day restricted the crowd to just over 8,000 but there was nothing wrong with the entertainment, with Wayne Clark heading the Everton goal and Allan Moore sliding in a Gary Mackay cross for the equaliser. Mackay took the scoring plaudits the next Saturday with an early strike that made a visit to Edinburgh difficult for Morton, and Kenny Black scored two further efforts to complete a comfortable win against Roddy McDonald and his mates.

Hearts by this time were setting the Premier Division pace and a 3-0 win at Motherwell on Wednesday 27 October stretched their lead at the top of the table to five points – an own goal, Wayne Foster and Robbo had been the killer blows for the Lanarkshire team.

More goals flowed against Dundee at home in a 4-2 win, courtesy of goals from Robertson (two), Colquhoun and Black, but then a visit by Celtic and failure to defeat the team rejuvenated by Billy McNeill's return to Parkhead, which was to prove so costly by the end of the season, was repeated. Mick McCarthy was sent off soon after half-time and it seemed that Hearts, already leading through a John Colquhoun goal, would claim the victory that would be so influential. But that man McGhee popped up again minutes from time to head the equaliser.

It had been a thrilling match, however, and if there was place for some sympathy for Alex MacDonald's players, there had to be admiration too for Celtic, who had played their part in providing fabulous entertainment for a capacity 29,000 crowd.

A goalless draw followed at Aberdeen and then a thrilling 3-0 win at Tannadice, with Robertson again on target twice and Wayne Foster providing the third, and as St Mirren prepared for a visit to Tynecastle on 21 November, Celtic had caught up with the games in hand and were just one point behind Hearts, with 20 matches played in an elongated season of 44 matches. As at

Aberdeen two weeks earlier, the goalkeepers were not beaten in the game against the Paisley side and there were few Sunday newspaper sub-editors who were able to resist the headline fact that Les Fridge in the St Mirren goal had stayed cool under tremendous pressure.

There were five goals, however, in Hearts' next match against Dunfermline at home, when Hearts found themselves 2-1 down with only six minutes left. Dave McPherson and Sandy Clark featured in the late, late show after John Robertson had seemingly started the night off perfectly with a tenth-minute header. The chairman, who was later to go on a much-publicised and successful diet, reckoned he started the whole procedure off that night, as the pounds poured off during the nerve-jangling second half.

That scoreline was repeated against Rangers at Ibrox on the last Saturday in November, but on this occasion Hearts were on the wrong end of the 3-2 result. Mike Galloway and John Robertson were the scorers, while at the other end Craig Levein had the misfortune of conceding an own goal.

A third win against luckless Falkirk came next although, after scoring nine goals in the previous two games, a John Robertson penalty was all that split the teams at full time, Stuart Romaines having hit the cross-bar two minutes from time. Then a sequence of five successive draws up to the New Year fixture with Hibs saw the team slip behind Celtic and Aberdeen in the league table. Mike Galloway and John Robertson scored in the first of these, a 2-2 draw at Celtic Park, and at Motherwell Gary Mackay's goal was cancelled out by Steve Cowan.

Dundee, Morton and Hibs were all tackled, the first two away from home, without a goal being scored, but all that inactivity ended with a vengeance at East End Park where Dunfermline were on the end of a 4-0 beating. Robertson scored two, Mike Galloway and John Colquhoun one each, and another fruitful sequence was started. Sandy Clark made sure the points were shared against Rangers at Tynecastle, and then in the Cup there were groans in plenty at Falkirk when they were paired with Hearts in the draw. Two goals from Robbo and one from John Colquhoun confirmed that their trepidation had been in order.

Mackay was an away scorer again as Dundee United failed for the third time that season to defeat the men in maroon in a 1-1 draw on Tayside, and there were six goals to drool over seven

Derby day high jinks

days later when St Mirren were visited in the league. It was to be Hearts' best ever away victory in the Premier Division and it was started, after 23 minutes, by a John Robertson penalty. By half-time, John Colquhoun had scored two more in a masterly display, and two minutes into the second half any chance of a Saints' revival were ended. Wayne Foster took full advantage of hesitancy in the Love Street defence to make it four, John Robertson added a fifth five minutes later and Colquhoun collected a marvellous hat-trick after an hour.

The second of three draws against Aberdeen was played out on 13 February and Jim Bett again gave Aberdeen the perfect early start from the penalty spot – Henry Smith pushed the kick on to the post, but Bett was first there to knock in the rebound. Robertson and Sandy Clark turned things round for Hearts but, with two minutes left, one of Ian Porterfield's English imports, Tom Jones, equalised from a hotly disputed penalty when Ian Jardine seemed to be in the way of the ball, rather than deliberately playing it.

Hearts stayed at home for the fourth round of the Cup against Morton, and were not unduly stretched by Alan McGraw's team. Sandy Clark lashed in a Robertson pass for the first and Gary

Mackay was next to accept Robbo's help, shooting high into the net from 20 yards, from a neat back-heeled pass by the striker.

Falkirk finally got the better of their tormentors at Brockville in the league at the end of February when Sam McGivern and Crawford Baptie were the main men for them in a 2-0 defeat, but at Motherwell there were better pickings through goals by Robertson and Colquhoun to keep the team in touch with the league leadership. Hearts' Cup fortunes were also good and in the fifth round Dunfermline fared little better than they had done in the league a few weeks earlier. This time the winning margin was restricted to three goals. John Colquhoun, Wayne Foster and Gary Mackay were the men who set up a semi-final date against Celtic at Hampden in April.

The final Edinburgh derby of the season was played at Easter Road before then, though, but the 0-0 draw did not end that season's series between the teams in an auspicious way. There were three straight wins coming up, however, that provided the perfect tonic en route to Hampden. Mike Galloway was on target twice against Morton - there was no reply from the Greenock team - and there was the same scoreline against Dundee thanks to goals from Kenny Black and John Colquhoun.

At Ibrox the following week, as talks over a new contract for Robertson became less and less convivial, Rangers were beaten thanks to a fine second-half performance after Jan Bartram needed a deflection to beat Henry Smith from 20 yards. Dave McPherson had the joy of scoring against his former club in the 66th minute to earn Hearts the platform to go for victory and this came seven minutes from the end. Gary Mackay was fouled in the box by goalkeeper Chris Woods . . . and Robertson rammed in the penalty. Celtic by this time had the championship ribbons all ready to tie, but only their most ardent fans could have held out much Cup hope, at the national stadium with three minutes of the semi-final left.

Hearts had been in the lead from the 60th minute after a first half that rarely threatened to produce a goal. When it did arrive the goal was an oddball effort, but for the Hearts' players, who had endured so many setbacks over the years, how it came to be in the net did not matter. Brian Whittaker floated in a cross from the right, aimed right under Packy Bonner's crossbar. As the Celtic 'keeper moved to grasp the ball, Dave McPherson went with him in the air and, distracted, Bonner lost the ball in flight and it dropped behind both players, amid joy and horror depending on which end you happened to be standing.

It seemed that the final beckoned, but with three minutes left the first of two cruel blows was to afflict the team. Henry Smith lost a cross in the air, and Mark McGhee drilled in the goal that took all the initiative away from Hearts and transferred it to Celtic. They needed no help as pressure mounted on Smith's goal and in the final agonising seconds Henry again took the blame, although McGhee's physical challenge in the air was vigorous. As the ball dropped, Andy Walker whipped it high into the net to end another dream.

There was another blow to come to terms with for the legions who trooped silently from Hampden Park that day, though. There now seemed a real possibility that John Robertson had played his last game for Hearts. Newcastle had been credited with a firm interest for some weeks, and when the man who had 31 goals to show for his efforts that season did not appear in the team that defeated Dunfermline 2-1 in the week after the Cup defeat, it seemed departure was imminent. Dave McPherson and Gary Mackay were the scorers in the Tynecastle win and, one week later, when Mackay and Galloway goals defeated Celtic 2-1 with Mark McGhee keeping up his incredible scoring record against Hearts, Wallace Mercer announced after the game that the club had accepted an offer of £750,000 for John. On Monday he would travel to St James' Park with his agent Bill McMurdo, and so straight were the talks that in less than an hour the pair were back on the road to Edinburgh, with the deal done and plans to house-hunt in the Morpeth area already in hand.

I spoke to John on his car-phone about the episode and, although both men were clearly and understandably delighted with the haste in which everything had been agreed, there could still be detected a feeling of uncertainty in his voice.

'After all these years there had to be some doubt, although I think one of the things that helped in that early period was being so close to Edinburgh. We had had contract talks, but there was no major shift on the club's part, so a move seemed the only way,' he explained. 'The great thing was that the split was amicable ... that was to be so important later when I came back to the club. Maybe we had just got too used to each other and I needed a change. Certainly, at that stage I could never have contemplated a return to Tynecastle. The first few weeks down there were frustrating, because with six games to go in the league programme and the matches all involving the top or bottom of the table, I couldn't play because I had signed after the transfer deadline, so that was disappointing. To make matters worse I pulled a stomach muscle during pre-season training and, after eight matches in the new season, I simply couldn't run. The answer was rest, and later that injury was to develop into a hernia.'

So the spell at Tyneside was not problem-free and the football grapevine was soon whispering misgivings about the whole move; a return to Scotland was certain. To where, was the question few could answer.

Alex MacDonald had always said that he would be delighted to have John back if the opportunity came along, but Dundee United manager Jim McLean was another interested party, while Rangers watched with interest also.

If the move south of the Border had been smooth and swift, the return to Edinburgh was bizarre. While Hearts were in far-off Mostar making sure of a place in the UEFA Cup quarter-final, Mercer was locked in talks with Newcastle. Willie McFaul had departed the manager's chair at St James' Park and in his place had moved Jim Smith, who had previously been with Queen's Park Rangers. He would meet John at the ground at 4.30 p.m., the day after the Mostar match.

The player told his gaffer that he wanted to stay on at Newcastle, regain his fitness, and fight for the first-team place he knew he could hold down. Smith was impressed. 'That's the kind of attitude I want here,' he concluded. The meeting was over.

Just two hours later John answered a telephone call from Smith dropping the bombshell news that he had been sold to Hearts, and the talks that had yielded nothing in the spring of that year would resume in Edinburgh.

There were no hitches, however, and John Robertson was back at the club he probably never should have been separated from. In some ways that's the way it appeared when he reported back for training on the Friday morning.

'Even to this day I still say the move was a good thing. The difficulties that the club and I had agreeing a deal could only have been resolved with a separation, so at the end of it all everyone was happy,' he suggested.

'Coming back into the club felt like I had never been away. That was in part down to the way Alex MacDonald ran the place.

The terrible trio – Scott Crabbe and John Colquhoun link up with Robbo

Everyone had their job to do, and everyone did it. So the routine I had grown up with was still very much in place.

'Sure, I took a bit of stick from some of the lads but that's to be expected with this bunch – they never miss an opportunity. But the novelty soon wore off, and it was just great to be there again. Tynecastle has a spirit about it that you get nowhere else.'

One thing missing from the scene was MacDonald's co-manager Sandy Jardine who was dismissed just before the away match in the UEFA Cup against Austria Vienna. The chairman was of the view that joint responsibility was not functioning and that a new direction was needed. MacDonald was to hear something similar just two years later. Also absent was director Douglas Park, who sold his shareholding to Mercer two days later, and who was alleged to be interested in leading boardroom opposition to the club chairman by that weekend. That was never confirmed and in any case never materialised. Jardine's place was taken by Walter Borthwick, who had been coach at the club since he joined Tony Ford in 1981, within weeks of Henry Smith coming on board, and Sandy Clark would join the coaching staff. In the boardroom, long-serving club secretary Les Porteous

Heads, not bottoms, for John Robertson and Jimmy Bone

became a director and later Hamish Deans, previously on the Motherwell board, joined Pilmar Smith and Bobby Parker as club directors.

So a period of upheaval had ended, but above all else the fans had found their man. They had Robbo back and frankly nothing else seemed to matter. However, the wee goal-machine would suffer months of frustration before the hernia was diagnosed and normal service was resumed.

The goals kept coming and, along with Scott Crabbe and John Colquhoun, he would soon be part of Scotland's top-scoring attack, as Hearts by this time were the only team in the country who would, week in, week out, employ three strikers in their formation. With the Cup gone in a few crazy minutes at Hampden, there was consolation in finishing second to Celtic in the championship, albeit by ten points. Rangers were two further behind in third, with Aberdeen three points adrift of Hearts.

After Robertson's move to Newcastle, Hearts ended their season drawing 0-0 at Pittodrie - the Dons had not beaten them all season - losing 1-0 against St Mirren at Tynecastle, and finishing the arduous campaign in another no-scoring affair against

Dundee United at Tannadice. It had been a strange season for Robertson. He had scored more goals than in any other and had left the only club he had served as a professional. If he was bemused by it all, he was well qualified to take the ups and downs, having listened many years ago to a snatch of fine advice from Jimmy Bone after a match when the young Robertson had hit one of the many hat-tricks in his career.

'Remember, wee man. A pat on the back is only two feet from a kick up the back side,' he told him in the dressing-room. Robertson has never forgotten.

CHAPTER NINE

Dave McPherson
1988-89

WHEN ALEX MacDONALD paid a club record £350,000 for David McPherson in the summer of 1987 it was a rare opportunity to indulge in this kind of transfer business . . . top class quality at a price Hearts could afford. Not that they had been in the business of spending that style of cash for years, but he convinced chairman Wallace Mercer that players of McPherson's ability crop up so rarely that the club should breach new financial parameters to get the player.

Where can you purchase, in that price range, a player who at the time was 23 and had experienced just about everything that the professional game could offer, and who, crucially, was an outstanding professional both on the pitch and off it? The answer, of course, is rarely, if ever, and McPherson's transfer remains a watershed in Hearts' progress from being a struggling, financially embarrassed team at the start of the Eighties to developing into one of the top teams in the country by the end of the decade.

With Rangers, McPherson knew what it was like to be a winner and he had already made significant strides, through Scotland's Youth and Under-21 teams, towards establishing for himself an international career which, only three years after Hearts' financial commitment, was to lead him to the World Cup finals in Italy.

One match which stands out in McPherson's memory during his formative years as an Ibrox player was, oddly, with the Scotland Youth Team in Mexico during the World Youth Championships, where Scotland had qualified under Andy Roxburgh by becoming European Champions for the first time ever. Indeed, when they won the European title during the finals in Finland in 1982, Gary Mackay, David Bowman and Ian Westwater had all been principal contributors to one of the most prestigious international performances by a Scotland team.

During the course of the tournament in Scandinavia I had been in regular daily contact with a colleague, Dick Donnelly. He was covering the competition for many of the newspapers in the country and the final in Helsinki came just 24 hours after the full Scotland international team had been beaten 1-0 by England in a disappointing Home International match at Hampden. Such was the gloom from Saturday's defeat that an international boost that was earned by the Youth team in far off Finland could not have been better timed. It was a pleasure for me to telephone the then Scotland manager, Jock Stein, with the news that the Youths had beaten Czechoslovakia 3-1 in Helsinki's Olympic Stadium. His excitement on hearing the outcome of the game was not born, however, out of any desire to see the national team's performance the previous day in a different light. No, simply, Jock was overjoyed that the nation should have achieved such a prestigious success.

McPherson was brought into the squad when they travelled to Mexico for the World Championships the following year, and he still recalls their final match in the qualifying section. Scotland met the host nation, Mexico, in the Aztec Stadium before 100,000 spectators, an astonishing attendance for a Youth International match, but par for the course in a country that supported that tournament with their normal, predictable fanaticism.

'Every game contains something to draw on with regard to experience, but the atmosphere and hostility in that stadium that spring evening was something quite remarkable,' recalled McPherson. 'Most of the players in the squad had experience at international level with previous Youth teams, and in many countries, including Scotland, there is tremendous support for the game at the younger level. But this was something else completely. The Mexicans sold out virtually every match for the competition, and the noise that night, coupled with the incredible humidity in the stadium, made it an intimidating place indeed. Going into that atmosphere and coming out with a victory gave every player in the side an inner belief in their ability to cope under pressure that can only be useful as your career continues.'

The season ahead was to provide the former Rangers man and his Hearts team-mates with the perfect opportunity to extend the level of their experience in matches outwith domestic competition to a greater degree than anyone looking ahead to the campaign could have appreciated. For Europe, and not Scotland's three premier competitions, was to provide Hearts with an unforgettable run in the UEFA Cup and, with the Edinburgh side having reached the quarter-finals in spring, allowed them the enjoyment and honour of being the last Scottish team in the three tournaments.

Unlike the match in season 1990/91 against Dnepr of the Soviet Union, the draw in Switzerland in July presented Hearts with a less arduous task in the opening round when they were paired with the part-timers of St Patrick's from Dublin. In order that the Irish club would derive maxium financial benefit from the first leg, that game was switched to Home Farm's Tolka Park, which from Hearts' point of view was fine, for it was on the airport side of the city and offered the perfect chance to travel back immediately after the game. The problem for MacDonald in this tie was to prepare the players and fans alike for the fact that no match in a European tournament would be easy, although of course Hearts were entitled, as favourites for the tie, to look toward round two with some optimism.

'Of course we had players of superior ability to the Irish team, but as everyone in football has known to their cost at some time or another, that is no guarantee for success. There are many other elements involved,' reflected MacDonald. 'One of the main problems was the pitch, which was very uneven, and at that stage in the season still fairly fiery, and with the Irish team being full of enthusiasm there was every chance this would be no stroll in the park.'

In the event, the outcome was predictable enough in front of 9,000 fans that included a contingent from Belfast who were apparently keen to cause problems. Prompt action by the Garda averted that threat. Hearts won 2-0 and made the tie virtually safe, with Mike Galloway netting a fierce downward header and Wayne Foster a penalty, to make the journey back over the Irish Sea a particularly enjoyable one. There is no truth to the rumour, I suspect, that chairman Wallace Mercer later fined the goal scorers on the basis that the crowd at Tynecastle for the second leg might have been affected by their outrageous efficiency.

The trip was not without the usual enjoyable Irish elements, as two players in particular were to find out at first hand. During the course of the second half Henry Smith went down with a cut head and was replaced by Murray McDermott who had been signed as cover for the first team 'keeper. However, in order to get Murray

The Irish Times – Mike Galloway on target against St Patrick's

on to the pitch Henry had to be removed from it, and that's where the delightful people who ran so successfully, in their own country, St Patrick's Athletic encountered some difficulty. As Henry lay on the pitch receiving treatment, the frantic search round the stadium for a stretcher - required of course by UEFA rules - went on. For more than five minutes the Hearts 'keeper could not be removed and the match was stopped. Happily, Henry's injury was not over-serious, although stitches were required and we were soon to hear the explanation. 'There was a fête on Saturday and we lent the organisers the stretcher. They forgot to bring it back,' offered a club official, still seemingly oblivious to the possibly serious nature of the omission.

Most of the lads enjoyed a beer after the match but for Walter Kidd that night the ale was forthcoming in strange and particularly rapid circumstances. 'Zico' had been selected as one of the players who would provide the post-match urine sample for drug-testing purposes. He couldn't . . . and half pints of ice-cold lager were summoned at frequent intervals from the pub at the corner of the street. Walter's test was negative and he enjoyed the sleep afterwards on the Aer Lingus chartered aircraft to Edinburgh.

The chairman's concern over the second leg attendance was perhaps justified on 5 October at Tynecastle when only 11,142

DAVE McPHERSON

Four to one – still good odds against Dundee

paid to watch yet another 2-0 victory and the clinching of a place in the second round. Even that attendance, considering the opposition and the state of the tie, was a considerable achievement. Galloway, who was to emerge as a prolific European scorer by any standards in any year during the campaign, was once again on the mark and Kenny Black was the other scorer in a match that was to see Hearts set a trend of keeping things immensely tight at the back.

The experience which McPherson had brought with him along the M8 to Tynecastle was a vast factor, for Hearts were tackling the UEFA Cup without the injured Craig Levein. However, Kidd, Neil Berry and Brian Whittaker were to emerge as tremendous aides.

From the quaint world of St Pat's the draw for the next round pitted Hearts against one of the Continent's most experienced teams, Austria Vienna, and sent them forth into one of Europe's legendary stadiums . . . the Prater Stadium in the Austrian capital.

Once again, the club elected to charter and as on previous occasions the man who put together the nuts and bolts of the trip was Ian Dunwoody of Travel Management (Group) from

It's neck and neck between Dave McPherson and Gareth Evans

Leamington Spa in Warwickshire. It seemed odd that the club should go so far geographically to enlist a company which would take care of the arrangements. The answer lies in the tremendous attention to detail that Dunwoody includes in his work. In the circumstances it was vital that everything was prepared meticulously so that management and players could concentrate fully on their task.

ADSCREEN

SCREEN PROCESS PRINTERS

250 Seaward Street, Kinning Park, Glasgow G41 1NG
Telephone: 041-420 1266 Fax No.: 041-420 1345

WE'RE PUTTING OUR SHIRTS ON HEARTS

WORLD CLASS

DAVE McPHERSON

McPherson – the athlete

It was true that the Austrians were not at this time regarded as one of Europe's great competitors. However, this was misleading. They were a club with a tremendous tradition and subsequent years are likely to show that Austrian football is in the throes of an upsurge that will make them a nation to fear in the Nineties.

The first leg at Tynecastle was typical of modern European ties. The Austrians were happy to contain at the back and hope to breach Hearts defence on the break, while the home players had a predictable dilemma to wrestle with. Yes, they wanted to pressurise their opponents and hoped to establish a tie-winning advantage from the home leg, but not at the expense of conceding their first goal in the tournament. In the event, chances were created but none taken and Hearts' run in the competition looked in real jeopardy.

More than 14,000 had watched the first leg and by the time the return came round two weeks later, on 9 November, the players had an additional difficult encounter as they prepared on the outskirts of Vienna for what would be an exceptionally taxing night. For even that early in the winter temperatures were below zero and the night before the match, when the players trained in the magnificence of the Prater, it became clear that underfoot conditions would be treacherous. No night surely for defenders to perform with comfort in an away leg, starting level.

After drawing in Edinburgh, the Austrians were making the expected noises in the circumstances. They still feared Hearts, and by no means regarded the tie as over. But secretly they were making a fatal error. A friend and colleague in Vienna, Lutz Lashki, telephoned me in the Vienna Hilton. 'I've been with the players and coaches and there is no doubt that they think the tie is over. They see no chance for Hearts to win away from home,' he confided.

As the game got underway, in freezing conditions, watched by 15,000 fans - of which 3,000 had journeyed from Edinburgh - a trend was very quickly set. Although Austria Vienna threatened Henry Smith a couple of times, the Kidd, Berry, McPherson and Whittaker combination was coping comfortably. And MacDonald had produced a tactical master-stroke in sending in young Jimmy Sandison to man-mark the over-confident home side's most influential player, the internationalist midfield man Herbert Prohaska. Sandison's ability to concentrate on the task and his quick, neat skills on a difficult surface kept the playmaker quiet and indeed pushed him back into his own half to an extent that Austria Vienna's ability to build threatening attacks was drastically diminished.

After 30 minutes of this ever encouraging performance, I tapped Jim Keen of the *Daily Record*'s shoulder as we sat in the Press Box. 'Hearts have a real chance, if this goes on,' I suggested. As a Scot watching a Scottish team abroad, optimism, and indeed occasional bias, were allowed even within the normal objective limits applied to media men. This judgement required no optimism and no bias.

A superbly flighted Eamon Bannon cross from the left was to accommodate the suggestion perfectly. His pass freed Walter Kidd on the right and, with the Austrians short of patience and pushing players forward recklessly, he was able to reach the bye-

Dave McPherson leans into his work

line for his final cross to be headed low into the net at the near post by Mike Galloway.

Our Austrian friends in the Press Box quickly claimed that Walter had been offside. Our group, which also contained Stewart Brown of the *Evening News*, Jim McLean of the *Daily Express* and Ian Wood of *The Scotsman*, argued the opposite case. That did, perhaps, require optimism and bias but nobody cared.

Hearts had reached the third round and by now it was clear that their sequence of four matches without conceding a goal was starting to breed a depth of confidence that could see them proceed even further in the tournament. The virtually unknown Velez Mostar, from Yugoslavia, would soon find out how firmly seated that confidence was.

As in the previous round, Hearts had been drawn at home first, not traditionally the way Scottish clubs prefer to tackle European ties but these matches are played in a different way now and the accustomed cavalry charge that accompanied the home leg was no longer appropriate. The precedent of not conceding a goal at home was to continue as the attendance figures at the Tynecastle UEFA Cup games - 17,417 watched the Velez tie - rose. The Yugoslavians, like St Pat's and Austria Vienna, were unable to find a way past Smith.

Amid a tremendous atmosphere, it was fitting that Bannon,

after so many years of ongoing success in Europe with Dundee United, should set the tone for victory with a low, left-foot drive. Mike Galloway collected the second and in a highly charged finale John Colquhoun drove in the third goal before going on to celebrate with the fans, trackside.

Three-goal victories in Europe are a rarity these days, but this one was absolutely crucial for Hearts. It virtually meant, if there were to be no disasters in the second leg, that interest in the season would be extended right through until March when the quarter-final stage would be Hearts' reward.

Considering what the club faced in terms of travel on the way to Russia in season 1990/91, the trip to Mostar was again to provide valuable experience for the players and for the backroom staff at the club, who once again excelled with pre-match preparations.

Mostar, a small picturesque town with a significant Turkish influence architecturally, sits high in the mountains overlooking the Adriatic, a four-hour coach journey from Split Airport where the team's charter craft was to land. From their earlier journeys to watch the team in action, Hearts were concerned over the standard of food in the available hotel in the town but made the necessary arrangements. Tim Kelly, of the Stakis Organisation, was brought in and the food for the club party travelled with him to be prepared in the hotel kitchens under his supervision.

There were hints at the hotel from the locals, who at times banged loudly on the hotel windows with their fists to create a menacing noise, that the atmosphere in the small stadium would not include the welcome you might expect from a town now firmly on the expanding Yugoslav tourist trail. The night was black as the game got under way and from the outset missiles, including coins, stones - some propelled from catapults - and bottles, flew from all corners of the pitch. Not many of them were directed at the Velez players.

David Francie and I were doing live commentary on the match for Radio Forth from a position on the trackside right on the halfway line, midway between the two dugouts. It turned out not only to be a poor vantage point for watching the game, but also a dangerous spot as the home fans decided that, if the tie was beyond them, some sort of victory was not. Glasses broke in front of us in the lanes of the athletic track that stretched to the touchline, and one bottle struck the roof of the Hearts dugout just seconds after Sandy Clark had sat down, showering fragments of glass everywhere.

Despite several players being struck, no action was taken by the officials, or the UEFA observer who claimed afterwards to have seen nothing, but happily, with Mike Galloway the goal scorer, the team eased comfortably into the last eight despite losing 2-1 on the night. The fact that Hearts were later fined by UEFA for encroaching on the track was quite staggering given the events of the night. But it was felt best to accept the punishment and rather to reflect on what had been a tremendous performance in difficult circumstances over the two legs.

The whole experience during the 90 minutes in Mostar had been memorable, then, for many reasons, but the drama of the night was not finished, as telephone calls from back home to the many journalists in the 30-strong party who travelled were soon to convey. The queries from the other side of Europe concerned a story that John Robertson was returning from Newcastle for £750,000. Vice-Chairman Pilmar Smith was unable to confirm the suggestion as we boarded coaches outside the match stadium bound for an overnight stay in Split and an early departure on Thursday morning. Wallace Mercer had, of course, stayed behind in Britain and later confirmation was received in the Adriatic resort that Tynecastle's favourite son had in fact returned after Newcastle had finally agreed to let him come back to Scotland. Several other Scottish clubs were interested and Mercer had to act quickly without the advantage of readily available contact with Alex MacDonald and his boardroom colleagues in Yugoslavia. The deal was done, though, and one of the most dramatic nights in the club's history was complete.

The domestic season had been just as lucrative in the early stages, although in mid-winter it became clear that coping with the heaviest workload in the Premier Division, because of those marvellous European performances, was proving difficult indeed.

After a six-game programme in West Germany which made up the bulk of the pre-season programme, Hearts enjoyed victories against Lossiemouth, Forres Mechanics, Airdrie and the Brazilians Cruzeiro in home friendlies that yielded 16 goals with just two against before the opening Premier Division match at Parkhead saw the season off to a disappointing start in a 1-0 defeat.

The Skol Cup was next and St Johnstone were despatched in the second round when an Iain Ferguson hat-trick was a feature of the 5-0 Tynecastle thrashing. Gary Mackay and substitute Ian Jardine were the other goal scorers. Meadowbank fell in the third round of the same tournament, with Kenny Black and Malcolm Murray the goal-getters, and there was another emphatic victory in the fourth round, when 15,500 fans watched Hearts defeat Dunfermline at East End Park 4-1. Ferguson was again among the goals with a pair. Colquhoun and Mackay hit the others before the Skol Cup trail ended abruptly against Rangers at Hampden. Just under 54,000 were in the national stadium and, although Hearts enjoyed good first-half spells, the goals just wouldn't come and Rangers finished comfortable 3-0 victors.

The Premier Division form in this spell after the Celtic defeat was mixed, for after a 3-2 home win against Hamilton - Colquhoun, Ferguson and Sandy Clark were on target - a no-scoring draw at Easter Road followed, before a Wayne Foster penalty was insufficient to avoid a disappointing 2-1 defeat at Love Street.

Four days before the Skol Cup defeat by Rangers, the Ibrox team had earned themselves the perfect tonic for the tie by winning 2-1 at Tynecastle where an own goal was Hearts' sole comfort. A single goal defeat by Aberdeen followed . . . and then Iain Ferguson earned a point at Dens Park.

While the European bandwagon had started to roll, points were still difficult to come by at home and after draws with Dundee United and Motherwell, the 2-0 home defeat by Celtic and a home 1-1 draw against Aberdeen straddled the first leg of the UEFA Cup-tie against Austria Vienna. Yet another defeat by Rangers - 3-0 again - this time at Ibrox, and an away point at St Mirren were followed by a derby defeat in early November by Hibs when Dave McPherson scored one of his five goals in the season from the back four.

No goals were scored when Dundee United visited Tynecastle and then the team went down 2-0 at Motherwell on the final Saturday in November, after the heady heights of the home leg against Mostar the previous Wednesday. The second leg was preceded by John Colquhoun's goal against Dundee at Dens, earning a draw, and on the two Saturdays after European progress to the quarter-final was ensured, successive 2-0 victories against Rangers and Hamilton at home seemed at last to have ended the trend. Mike Galloway and Iain Ferguson scored against the Ibrox team and seven days later McPherson and Alan McLaren were on target.

But still the in and out nature of results continued for, despite

Dave McPherson gets the scoring end right

John Robertson's first goals since returning from the North-east of England, Hearts were beaten 4-2 by Celtic at Parkhead on Hogmanay and the New Year celebrations were indeed muted after a second defeat in the season by Hibs, by a single goal at Easter Road on 4 January.

Four points were then gathered from three matches against St Mirren, Motherwell and Dundee United, without conceding a goal, as it became clear that a place in Europe again the following season was in real jeopardy through a League placing if the Scottish Cup were not to yield qualification for the Cup Winner's Cup.

That competition was started with a comfortable victory over Ayr United in the third round, when McPherson, Galloway and Colquhoun and an own goal featured in a 4-1 victory. Partick Thistle were defeated 2-0 in the next round, courtesy of goals from Colquhoun and Bannon.

In the League, Mackay, Colquhoun and Bannon all found the Dundee net at Tynecastle in a 3-1 victory but as the club prepared for one of the biggest nights in its 150-year history - against mighty Bayern Munich at Tynecastle - there was a numbing 3-0 defeat at Pittodrie, serving as a brutal reminder that Europe was once again taking a massive toll on domestic performances.

Hearts had, of course, been the last Scottish club in the three European competitions since round two had been completed and, understandably, prices for the quarter-final tie were dramatically increased. But crucially, regular Hearts fans were cushioned by way of a voucher system operated at previous matches.

The West Germans, who have over three decades earned the right to be considered one of Europe's top five clubs, had style to go with their impressive pedigree. They were to stay in Edinburgh's Sheraton, and while the players flew in, the team coach they use all over the world was shipped into Scotland to accommodate their travel in and around the city. The Germans had a wonderful record across Europe, holding the distinction of winning the European Champions' Cup on three occasions in the Seventies, defeating Atletico Madrid in a replayed final, Leeds United and then St Etienne in Hampden Park's second opportunity to stage that prestigious game. They possessed continuity as well, for Ule Hoeness collected winners' medals in all three games and was now general manager when Bayern arrived in the Capital.

They came to the match in the kind of form that had earned them such eminence in the Seventies, with superb West German internationalists in Klaus Augenthaler and Olaf Thon, while up front the personality player was the great Swede, Johnny Ekstrom. In the first round Thon had scored twice when they defeated Legia Warsaw in Munich before they travelled to Poland and slammed seven goals past the bemused Poles - Ekstrom scored twice and even defender Augenthaler was on target. Round two once again took them behind the Iron Curtain to face Czechoslovakia's Dunajsta Streda. After winning 3-1 at home - Thon was again a marksman - they indicated their comfort at difficult away venues, with another victory by the same margin. Thon scored both goals in the 2-0 win.

While Hearts were going to one of football's outposts in Mostar in the third round, Bayern's current well-being was being tested to the maximum in the tie of the round against Inter Milan. The first, in the Olympic Stadium in Munich, was goalless but the overall tie took on a dramatically gloomy hue when goals from Serena and Berti made the journey, in their customised coach for the second leg, a trip laced with danger. Incredibly, the Germans turned the whole thing round with three goals inside six first-half minutes and, although Serena pulled one back for Inter, they had progressed on the away goals rule . . . and it was Tynecastle next stop.

The atmosphere inside Tynecastle stadium proclaimed one simple truth . . . this was the big time. 26,294 filed into the ground for Hearts' biggest home attendance of the season and every breath on the terraces, and in the stand, held fevered anticipation.

Like the Austrians in the second round, Bayern, with Jupp Heynckes as their coach, were supremely confident of going through into the semi-finals. Heynckes, like Hoeness, had been a West German internationalist of great standing and indeed Alex MacDonald remembered playing against him for Rangers, against Bayern.

But as the match progressed it soon became clear that the Germans, although free-scoring in the earlier rounds, could also be breached in defence, as the eight goals they had conceded in the same number of previous ties indicated. Hearts made opportunities and had pressure to repel as well, but as the game went into the second half it was clear there was precious little between the teams. It was perhaps not surprising that a set-piece was needed to provide the breakthrough.

The free-kick was for Hearts, ten minutes into the second half, and the position 22 yards out from goal, just left of centre. The Germans pulled every player back into the penalty area and lined up a formidable wall in front of goalkeeper Raimond Aumann. As if to heighten the tension, there was a brief delay before Tosh MacKinlay and Iain Ferguson stood over the ball. MacKinlay cleverly moved the ball two yards to the right and then quickly flicked the ball, right again, into Ferguson's path, creating a better angle for the final shot.

The forward, who had with Dundee, Rangers and Dundee United over many seasons created a well-earned reputation for being one of the fiercest strikers of a dead ball in the Scottish game, did not let the legions of Hearts fans down. Arcing his run into the ball slightly from the left to acquire the position from which to put some curl on the kick, his blistering right-foot drive swept past the Bayern defence to their left and, although Aumann leapt quickly enough to his right, the ball flew into the net a couple of feet inside the post.

Rarely can a goal have been received with such ecstasy in a Hearts match. Amid jubilation and tears the tense match failed to produce a further goal, which would have influenced the tie so much for either side, and two weeks later the issue would be decided.

If the Prater Stadium in Vienna, with its cold, grey concrete structure, conjured up great matches from the past, Munich's Olympic Stadium with its futuristic covering held a menace that still somehow was captured in the present.

Strangely, there were only 25,000 at the game but for Hearts that was no bad thing. The crowd in the vast bowl was set back by the athletics track, some way from the playing surface, so any intimidation that may have poured from the towering terraces was minimised. In any case, the thousands of Hearts fans were making a pretty good job of being heard. Strolling on to the magnificent playing surface before the game, with the players and club officials, there was an unfailing feeling of confidence that they could play out the second leg and, whatever the result, they could return to Edinburgh knowing they had let no one down.

It was no shock to find the home team earning more of the ball for themselves than they had done in Edinburgh, but there was encouragement and optimism in the realisation that they weren't getting to Henry Smith with any great regularity in the early stages of the game. MacDonald had stressed frequently to his players the menace of Augenthaler when the defender pushed forward in support of his front players. In fairness, the warning had been heeded and he was quickly closed down whenever he threatened danger.

These bright, opening minutes, however, succumbed to despair after just a few seconds more than a quarter of an hour had been played. Augenthaler again crept into the Hearts half . . . the ball was played square in front of him . . . and MacDonald's vision appeared in stark reality as his searing right-foot shot swept high past Smith.

It was the worst possible scenario but, after the Edinburgh side had weathered a spell of sustained pressure, John Colquhoun sped over the halfway line and his pace and one-touch took him clear of Erland Johnsen's final challenge. He trailed them all to just outside the penalty area, and caught his right-foot drive with perfect power . . . it was low, and sadly two feet wide of the post. From the stands it seemed as if a golden opportunity had been missed. Quick reference to a television replay swiftly indicated however that the tiny striker's effort had been perfectly placed, and only Aumann's outstretched right hand had stood between

Hearts and a crucial away goal.

That would have been hard enough for Colquhoun to accept on its own, but there was even more misery to cope with in the second half as Bayern's players and supporters became increasingly nervous of conceding an equaliser that would dump them out of the competition. And it was to Colquhoun once again that the disappointment would fall. Kenny Black lifted a corner from the right into the penalty area and it fell beyond the tall player's reach at the near post. Astoundingly, John had found space deep in the heart of the box, but there was only time for an instinctive head glance.

Aumann was a spectator, as were the Bayern markers, but the goalkeeper's right-hand post seemed, for a fraction of a second, to be a foot wide as the ball smacked off and bounced back to Dave McPherson, whose fierce drive cannoned off Johnsen to complete an incredible let-off.

Minutes later, to confirm that the one snatch of luck which was all that separated the teams would not belong to the Edinburgh players, Bayern broke clear on the right and, although there was a real suspicion of offside when Reuter's initial pass was played through, the flag stayed down and defender Johnsen's outstretched leg stabbed in an untidy goal for the Germans.

It is always hard to recall the many memorable moments on the way to a mountainous disappointment but Hearts fans managed, as the players trooped disbelievingly from the pitch. They were given a fitting reception in and outside the stadium after a magnificent campaign. It was no consolation on the night, which ended with some unfortunate remarks from Heynckes over the style which Hearts had used to force them to within a hair's breadth of defeat, but he, like everyone who watched the 180 minutes of absorbing football, would know the truth. Hearts, mere fledglings in European terms compared to one of the giants of world football, had been every bit as good as them, both home and away. Not even the scoreline could steal that crucial realisation away from MacDonald and his players.

It would have been a fitting compliment to their efforts if Bayern had gone forward to win the competition, by way of franking their performance, but Diego Maradonna's Napoli ended that notion in the semi-final with a 4-2 victory. However, the Italians did win it, defeating Stuttgart in the two-leg final by the odd goal in nine.

Despite his anger at the after-match press conference remarks, MacDonald could not hide his pride in the players, many of whom had just two European ties in their system before the season's lengthy campaign. 'They were magnificent. No more could have been asked from them . . . at the end of it all we were an inch away from the semi-final,' he insisted.

Inevitably, there was an element of the Lord Mayor's show in what was contained in the domestic season, for sandwiched between the two UEFA Cup quarter-final matches was a single goal defeat by Celtic at Tynecastle. The Parkhead side also ended Hearts' interest in the Cup four days after the Munich match when Eamonn Bannon was the goal scorer in Glasgow. Hamilton were then defeated at Douglas Park where McPherson and Mackay hit the goals while Bannon and Robertson were on target against Hibs at Tynecastle in a day of consolation and reward for the fans.

Maintaining consistency was still a problem in the League, however. This time it was a defeat at Dens and a draw at Love Street which illustrated the problem but with four weeks of the season left hopes of a return to Europe were heightened against Aberdeen at Tynecastle, when Mike Galloway headed in Tosh MacKinlay's cross to end the Dons' slim championship hopes. Just seven days later, two goals each from Mel Sterland and Kevin Drinkell at Ibrox were final proof that the players had given their all, physically and mentally, on pitches a long way distant from the Premier League venues. Mind you, there was still enough resilience to earn closing draws against Dundee United and Motherwell.

Away from the first team, though, the Tannadice team were to feature in another night to remember, when 4,454 watched the reserve team defeat Dundee United at Tynecastle to win the Reserve League Cup. Scott Crabbe's undiluted joy as he held the trophy aloft was a clear hint of what was to come from him. They had upstaged the big boys, for despite so much effort and enjoyment, there was nothing tangible to take away from a remarkable season except further proof, at the very highest level, of MacDonald's judgement when the big cheque was written for McPherson the previous summer.

In April, McPherson had been called into the Scotland squad to meet Cyprus in a World Cup qualifying tie at Hampden after Gary Gillespie had once again found injury frustrating his international ambitions. The Scots won 2-1, and he became the 59th Hearts player to play for his country. Two years on, in Italy, he was to prove conclusively his ability to compete on that stage. Who would bet against him topping Tommy Walker's record of 29 appearances to become the club's most capped player?

CHAPTER TEN

Henry Smith
1989-90

HENRY SMITH is well used to being patient, going right back to the time as a 21-year-old when he took his first surprise steps into professional football. And his work as a coalface miner in Yorkshire steeled him against disappointment.

Many goalkeepers are notorious for developing late. Henry had almost accepted that his working life would be spent down the pit, and he would settle for the great enjoyment he took from amateur football. That was until the influence of Jimmy Adamson was to guide his future. Henry's amateur side, Winterton, had won a Birmingham five-a-side competition involving teams from all over England. The first prize was a set of floodlights, and Sheffield Wednesday had agreed to provide the opposition for the opening ceremony.

It was in that week that Henry's career was to take off. The back page of his local evening newspaper proclaimed: 'WINTERTON 'KEEPER SIGNS FOR SUNDERLAND'. The former Burnley great, Jimmy Adamson, was manager at Roker Park and had watched the young Smith improve his game in the amateur ranks. He moved quickly to arrange trials for Henry before Wednesday had the chance to see him at close quarters. The trials worked out well and Henry Smith was able to go home to his miner dad and break the good news that he had been offered terms.

For Smith senior, the chance to watch his son break away from generations in mining was a heaven-sent opportunity, and notice to quit at the mine was quickly in place, but 24 hours later came an even stranger telephone call . . . Henry was to travel to Leeds and discuss a signing proposition at Elland Road. The reason behind this strange turn of events – when, after months of hoping his chance would come, without any real interest from the many senior clubs around, two clubs suddenly wanted him inside 48 hours – was that Jimmy Adamson had been sacked at Sunderland and appointed manager at Leeds.

Henry knew from the first moment that first-team football, especially in a team which was suffering from a reaction to the great Don Revie days, would be difficult. The competition ranged before him were Scottish internationalists David Harvey and Dave Stewart.

'I worked away in the reserves and for a while was in awe of many of my team-mates. At this time, we were still talking of people like Eddie Gray, Norman Hunter, Peter Lorimer and Trevor Cherry, but the big problem was lack of help for a young goalkeeper. I felt there was no one prepared to take me aside and point out errors, far less suggest ways of correcting them. However, I still felt there were times when I had done enough to merit a chance.'

Both Harvey and Stewart were edging toward the end of their first-team careers, indeed Smith played in Harvey's testimonial match, but the situation began to look bleak again when a young man called John Lukic arrived on the scene. He quickly took over the first-team spot and, even though he was prone to the errors that have punctuated his career, he managed to keep Henry's challenge for a first-team place at bay.

If Lukic was to prove a difficult barrier to his ambitions, there was even more formidable competition to arrive when Leeds signed a youngster called David Seaman, who, like Lukic, has featured in the big money transfers in 1990.

If all this conspired to make Smith's task difficult, there was worse to follow, for the man who had been so adamant that he had what it took to succeed, Jimmy Adamson, was sacked. Without a friend in the manager's office, a phone call to the National Coal Board looked inevitable, especially when former Leed's striker, Alan Clarke, took over as manager, and quickly decided that there would be no first-team football for Smith. Mind you, that was not to evolve as the most painful snub in football history for, using the best judgement of goalkeepers he could muster, he sold Lukic and Seaman as well as Smith and deprived, in the fullness of time, the Leeds treasurer of a seven-figure sum of money.

The application form for the pit was dusted down and had, in fact, been posted when the chance to join Hearts in the summer of 1981 during a pre-season trip to the north of England came up. He played a half-match in two of the friendly games and, having met manager Tony Ford and new chairman, Wallace Mercer, quickly accepted their invitation to move to Edinburgh. One of the best bargains of the Eighties was struck.

Over the years, the now 34-year-old Smith has proved himself to be one of Scotland's most reliable and consistent goalkeepers and Clarke's suspect judgement surely received the final blemish when a full cap against Saudi Arabia in 1988 was the final accolade. That international promotion came after a number of appearances on the Scotland bench.

Patience and resilience, then, have been Smith's hallmark, and he is adamant that the trophy Tynecastle fans craved so much will still arrive at the Edinburgh ground.

'Every single season our squad has improved and with the experience they have gathered over the years, I am certain that Hearts can go one better and that it will happen quickly,' he insisted. 'The League and Cup double failure was a devastating blow for everyone, but our players have been through that now and if the same set of circumstances arose again, I am certain they would not be found wanting.'

There have been many great moments for Smith in his nine seasons with Hearts, but there is a good case for saying that the 1989/90 campaign, which saw him ever-present in competitive games, was his best ever. All the experience that maturity brings was in evidence as Hearts battled to a place in the top three, when only goal difference shaded Aberdeen in front of them for the runners-up place.

Recalled Smith, 'In hindsight you look at two home defeats by Dunfermline, an away defeat at St Mirren, points dropped against Dundee in two matches, and other slips that we paid dearly for. These were the results that let us down and not our performance against the teams at the top end of the Premier Division. We get closer to them every season. It's the consistency that champions need that Hearts have to perfect.'

The start of the season had seen manager MacDonald recruit three new players to further strengthen his squad. From Yugoslavia came the tall striker Husref Musemic, from Red Star Belgrade and, although the likeable Slav's contribution to the club was limited in terms of time, he will always be remembered by Hearts fans for heading the only goal of the first derby in the season against Hibs at Tynecastle in late August.

'Husref was a tremendous character and tried his best to adjust

Official supplier of **Heart of Midlothian F.C.**
lottery tickets

Wishbone Print (Birmingham) Limited

Registered Office
Wishbone House, Bradford Street, Birmingham B12 0NS
Telephone 021-773 0181
Fax 021-772 6215

Registered in England No. 1375448

It's a windy day for Henry Smith

both socially and in a playing sense,' recalled MacDonald. 'But like so many players from the Continent, he was not found lacking in natural ability, but simply could not meet the physical demands in our Top Ten. He wanted to play the ball outside the penalty area and make runs into positions where he could use his height. We needed a striker who could take the pressure in the penalty box and the big man simply wasn't that type of player.'

MacDonald also raided Ibrox yet again, in the hope that for £100,000 David Kirkwood would provide competition in midfield, having failed to cope with the big name environment at Rangers following his transfer from East Fife. A versatile player, David was able to slot into the left full-back position early in the season and use the intelligent long passes that are a feature of his game, from midfield. Finding the consistency of performance that would make him a first-team regular has still eluded him however.

Some weeks into the season the third new acquisition arrived at Tynecastle and it's true to say that no one at the club has properly recovered from the experience. Irishman David McCreery was to bring with him, after a short stint in Sweden, all the wit and wisdom that had made him one of the English game's most endearing characters in spells, notably with Manchester United,

Queen's Park Rangers and Newcastle. The little midfield player has over 70 caps for Northern Ireland to his credit and had the thrill of being an integral part of the Irish team which made such an indelible mark on the 1982 World Cup. His input in his first season at Hearts is impossible to measure.

Added MacDonald, 'He's a tremendous character and there's no doubt that, as a club, Hearts will lean on David's experience and ability to lift the place as long as he's here. It's like New Year every morning meeting David McCreery.

'Mind you, he was almost a very expensive signing for there was a time when I thought I might have to hire an interpreter to unscramble his machine-gun delivery. A conversation with Davy and big Husref was something to behold. It usually ended with a shrug of the shoulders from the big fellow.'

The start of the season was not without its difficulties, however, for John Robertson, who had arrived back from Newcastle the previous winter, had still not solved his stomach muscle problem during the close season. It was discovered that a hernia had been causing the difficulties and although surgery was applied immediately, it meant that the striker would not be seen in first-team activity until the final days of August against Celtic in the Skol Cup.

For midfield player Neil Berry the problem was the opposite. He had arrived ready for the new campaign, rejuvenated from a summer's hard work, but that all ended with a painful foot injury at Brockville in mid-August, during a fiery Skol Cup third-round match. He was to miss the entire winter, not reappearing until late February in a Scottish Cup match against Motherwell.

These two fairly lengthy absences, combined with the normal knocks and strains that inevitably accompany Premier League combat, meant that finding a settled side for a campaign that looked to promise so much was no easy matter. Neverthless, the opening stages of the season contained no shortage of encouragement after the disappointment of an opening day defeat by Celtic had worn off.

The team travelled to that Tynecastle setback via pre-season victories over Nairn County, Inverness Caley, Peterhead and Sunderland, before Russian tourists Dynamo Tbilisi took advantage of a hectic five games in 11 days schedule, winning 2-0 at Tynecastle.

Dave McPherson underlined that his talents include goal

Big 'H' – going into his second decade

scoring in that first competitive game against Billy McNeill's team, but a hat-trick from Tommy Coyne, often a problematical customer for Hearts, sent the Glasgow team into the new season with the best possible tonic.

In the Skol Cup four days later, MacDonald's players went into their first tie in the competition with memories of a horrific defeat by Montrose a couple of years earlier. They were determined to make certain there would be no repeat. The 3-0 scoreline was a nice lift following the Celtic defeat but, much more importantly, the two goals scored by Scott Crabbe were the first signs that MacDonald had found a new talent from within the ranks.

The youngster had been at Tynecastle for five seasons and, although he had threatened on many occasions to break through from his midfield position in the reserve team, the switch up front was to suit him perfectly. Crabbe was also not the first player to benefit from extra summer work at Meadowbank with sprint coaches Bert Logan and George McNeill. He arrived at the new season stronger and quicker than ever before.

Musemic was the other scorer in a comfortable Skol Cup victory, and the Yugoslav found the target again at Love Street against St Mirren when Neil Berry was the other goal scorer at a venue that had on occasion in the past provided problems for Hearts teams.

The Berry injury occurred the following midweek when Hearts comfortably withheld Falkirk's challenge to reach the quarter-final of the Skol Cup. That night at Brockville provided a happy memory for Walter Kidd. So often there had been challenges to his first-team status, but the former club captain scored one of the goals in a 4-1 win in which Crabbe, Kirkwood and Eamonn Bannon were the others to earn the victory.

It was Musemic, whose close-in header sent home-fans into ecstasy in the first derby match, as Smith kept goal in the first of four Premier Division meetings with the city rivals, that was to see Hearts emerge undefeated in a sequence in which the goalkeeper was beaten only twice.

It seemed that the Skol Cup might present Hearts with the route toward the trophy which their consistency over the years had deserved, even though their quarter-final opponents were Celtic, again at Tynecastle, in a fixture which represented a swift opportunity to avenge the first day of the season. In a midweek match watched once again by more than 25,000 fans, Crabbe scored once and Robertson emerged from the bench for his first appearance of the season to grab the honour. But not even extra time could separate the teams in an exhilarating two hours that would stand amongst the most watchable matches of the entire season. Penalty kicks were needed to separate the teams but, while Celtic were clinical and accurate from the spot, Hearts' efforts were sufficiently unsuccessful to avoid Gary Mackay taking the final shoot-out kick. Another Cup run was ended.

League points would now be the priority, for without Europe after the heady delights of the previous season, only the Scottish Cup after the turn of the year would offer Hearts the chance of tangible success.

Two awkward away fixtures in the opening fortnight of September against Dundee and Motherwell would test Hearts' ability to be championship contenders and there was understandable optimism when the three hours' football yielded three points. Dave McPherson collected his second goal of the season in a 2-2 draw at Dens and Scott Crabbe's penalty saw him continue to set a blistering pace in the race to see who would emerge as the club's top scorer. At Fir Park the following week, Crabbe scored twice but Robertson, fast catching full fitness, grabbed the other for his second goal in three matches - ample warning that he was not about to give up his long-held reputation as Hearts' top finisher.

McPherson was the scorer again in a disappointing 1-1 home draw with Dundee United, before Alex Ferguson's Manchester United were to fill in a blank European club competition week in a testimonial match for Eamonn Bannon. When the player who had started his career at Tynecastle in the Seventies returned to Edinburgh from Dundee United the previous summer, he was to miss a Tannadice testimonial. Hearts were happy to take over that responsibility for a player who had been sold to Chelsea a decade earlier in a bid to rescue ailing club finances. United won 4-2 in the event, but Bannon himself scored from the penalty spot and MacDonald used the opportunity to introduce several fringe players against opponents of the highest quality. Over 9,000 watched the match, which was a fitting tribute to one of Scotland's most respected players both at club and international level.

A first visit to Ibrox followed and, despite a performance that left most observers with the impression that there was nothing between the teams, Hearts travelled back along the M8 victims of a single goal defeat. However, worse was to follow at home just four days later.

Dunfermline, under the effervescent Jim Leishman, were having a second attempt at avoiding a quick return to Division One and, if they had been a little cavalier in their previous Premier League season, reality now intruded into Leishman's approach.

Peter McCloy - the coach

The result was a night of frustration for Hearts. Ross Jack, who was to push Robertson right to the last day of the season as the Premier Division's top scorer, found the net twice in rare intrusions into an evening of Hearts dominance, when a solitary reply from substitute Musemic was little comfort to a stunned 14,000 crowd.

Solace was at hand five days later, but the faithful had to make the long journey to Aberdeen to watch the players make good some of the damage that had been inflicted by the team from Fife. Crabbe was once again the man who accepted the scoring honours with two goals, but if the match was to feature Tosh McKinlay's only successful strike of the season, the full-back could hardly have done it more spectacularly. A rising, curling, left-foot volley from just outside the penalty area flashed behind Theo Snelders in the Aberdeen goal to thrill BBC Scotland's viewing audience that night.

A third attempt to overcome Celtic ended in failure at Parkhead the following week when Crabbe struck once, but couldn't halt the Parkhead side on their way to a 2-1 victory. However it was that weekend that John Robertson gave himself a very personal target that would see him emerge as the country's top scorer. Although

154

just over two months of the season had been completed, Crabbe by this time had found the net on 11 occasions while Robbo had only that single goal against Celtic in the Skol Cup to commend his efforts. That did not stop him from challenging the young pretender in a goal-scoring contest over the full season that would carry with it the magnificent sum of £5 for the winner.

There were several suggestions that a fiver was enough to turn Robertson into some kind of superman, but whatever the truth of that he was to start clawing back the deficit in an impressive 4-0 victory over St Mirren the following week when he scored twice, Crabbe only once and John Colquhoun reminded everyone that, although they had to be patient for his first goal of the season, he was not about to allow this side-show to become a two-man affair.

Ahead of the second derby of the season, watched by more than 19,000 spectators at Easter Road, manager MacDonald was being irked by the criticism that had been levelled at recent matches between Hearts and Hibs, for there was no doubt that the fear of defeat in such an important city fixture had become a big factor. 'We have to bear in mind that the pressure on both teams is immense. The supporters want to see their team win this fixture so much that, of course, that transmits itself to the players,' he suggested. 'We never went into any match, either at home or away, without being fully committed to winning the game and using three forwards to achieve that. However, a point at Easter Road is an away point in a difficult League match, and counts exactly the same as a point at any other venue.'

Like Colquhoun the previous week, Bannon was to shoot his first Premier Division goal at Easter Road that afternoon and if that had been poor reward for the degree of possession Hearts had enjoyed, the goals were to flow with an incredible fourish in the following two matches.

Colquhoun grabbed a hat-trick as Dundee fell 6-3 at Tynecastle in a match that contained comic moments as well as superb skill and flair, and while Wayne Foster and Robertson scored from their place in the starting line-up, Crabbe replaced Gary Mackay in the second half to keep tabs on Robertson in their own private duel.

He was to do even better the following Saturday when he, Colquhoun and Jimmy Sandison sent three goals past Motherwell at Tynecastle before two successive defeats would deal a deadly

'Where is it, Andy?' asks Wayne Foster

blow to Hearts' hopes of staying with the championship race. A Scott Crabbe penalty at Tannadice was insufficient to take anything from a visit to United and, although Bannon earned them a December lead against Rangers, the Ibrox men persisted to earn their second victory of the season over the Tynecastle team, this time at home.

By this time McCreery had been through his introduction to the Premier Division and, although he admitted that the pace was hectic, he was enjoying his first taste of Scottish club football other than matches he had played north of the border with English teams over the years.

'There's nothing like the same amount of time on the ball as you get in the English leagues, but the fans clearly love it and that's got to be important. One thing is for sure, there's a marvellous family atmosphere at Hearts and I'm convinced, like the rest of the players at Tynecastle, that the day when a trophy will be in the boardroom is not far off.

'There's a tremendous wealth of young talent at the club and I am amazed that this is Scott Crabbe's first full season as a regular. He's developed tremendously quickly as a front player, and looks as comfortable as any striker I've seen at the top level. Alan McLaren, for a 19-year-old, is another who has tremendous scope

Scott Crabbe – under and out

for the future and it's up to us, the more experienced players, to help these boys and others along,' he observed.

McCreery's perceptive appraisal of the opening few months of the season soon proved to be spot on as Hearts embarked on a spell that saw just one away defeat at St Mirren mar an otherwise undefeated spell of ten matches. The first six in that sequence saw

Hearts score only six times, mind you, but a pattern was being set with Robertson claiming five of them. There were two for the striker in the 2-0 win at Dunfermline, one at home in a 1-1 draw with Aberdeen, no goals as Hearts and Celtic fought it out in a goalless stalemate at Tynecastle, and obviously none in a 2-0 Love Street defeat. But the irrepressible Robertson was on target again when Hibs called on New Year's Day. Two more goals were his haul, one from the penalty spot, and, after an own goal earned both points at Dens Park on 6 January, Robertson went on to claim two more in a 3-0 win at Motherwell when Colquhoun was the other scorer.

On 20 January the Scottish Cup campaign was underway when, like the Skol Cup in the autumn, the ballot paired Hearts with Falkirk, this time at Tynecastle. The 2-0 scoreline underlined a comfortable enough afternoon for MacDonald and his players, and inevitably Robertson scored both goals.

One week on, and Robertson and Crabbe took one each from the 3-2 victory over Dundee United, when Walter Kidd had Hearts in front with a strange goal in the opening minute. His persistence took him to the United byeline, and when his cross was met by Alan Main at the near post, the United 'keeper could only palm the ball into the corner. 'Magnificent vision,' commented Kidd, modestly, after the match.

Incredibly, with February round the corner, Robertson, with the sight of the blue £5 note driving him on incessantly, had cut the gap to just one goal. He had scored 15 and Scott Crabbe 16 as the youngster was placed under pressure for the first time in the season.

The following Saturday at Aberdeen, in a 2-2 draw, Crabbe and Jimmy Sandison were to embark on samba-style celebrations at Pittodrie, after the midfield player had drilled in a 20-yard drive that was to make the back pages of all the Sunday newspapers and feature whimsically on television. Iain Ferguson scored the other Hearts goal.

The strikers had two barren weeks in yet another crushing home defeat by Dunfermline - 2-0 the margin this time - and a no-scoring draw at Ibrox when, as in the autumn fixture at Rangers' ground, the Hearts players travelled back convinced they had done enough to have earned victory.

Scottish Cup hopes were raised once again seven days later. Hearts whipped four goals past Motherwell in the fourth round at

Tynecastle, with two goals from Robertson and one each from Colquhoun and Crabbe. The bookmakers now saw fit to shorten their odds for the national trophy to 5/1. That optimism would not be diminished in the two subsequent games.

Motherwell returned on League business and fared better this time, losing only 2-0, with Robertson and Crabbe scoring one each, and then Robbo drew level with his front-line partner in the 1-1 draw at Parkhead. There was nothing to suggest that the cruellest disappointment of the season was round the corner, at Aberdeen in the quarter-final of the Cup.

It was, of course, an immensely difficult draw, against a team who had established a tremendous Cup tradition throughout the Eighties, but there was a feeling throughout the country that Hearts could succeed that March afternoon and perhaps go on to win the Scottish Cup. In a performance that is still difficult to understand, John Colquhoun briefly gave Hearts hope close on half time, but Aberdeen finished easy 4-1 winners and the journey back to Edinburgh was a long, tedious three hours indeed.

'Defeat is always difficult to accept. Every team has to deal with that from time to time . . . but this was something different,' suggested Henry Smith. 'There are not many times when we can confess that we let ourselves down, but that day at Pittodrie we did.

'Even now, it's impossible to explain away. Our preparation had been tremendous and everything had gone smoothly. Quite simply, too many players didn't produce their best on the day, and Aberdeen were to remind us that on their pitch you just don't get away with that.'

The remainder of the season consisted of chasing Rangers, who by this time had established what appeared to be an invincible lead at the top of the table, but second place in the championship was a distinct possibility with Aberdeen again the adversaries.

Two no-scoring draws against St Mirren and Dundee at Tynecastle straddled another derby victory at Easter Road when John Robertson, who has been so hard on Hibs over the years, was a two-goal man once again on the ground where he had trained as a youngster. Dave McPherson earned a 1-0 victory against Dunfermline at East End Park, Gary Mackay scored his only goal of the season to defeat Aberdeen at Tynecastle and Alan McLaren found the net at Tannadice in a 1-1 draw before Rangers brought the curtain down on a season when goal difference favoured Aberdeen, and Hearts settled for third place. In the final 1-1 draw with the champions, fittingly Robertson, from the penalty spot, was the home scorer.

That final League position of course contained with it a guarantee of a place in the UEFA Cup draw in Switzerland in July, and not even the news that Hearts were given an awkward first round tie against Dnepr from the Soviet Union could dampen enthusiasm for a return to Europe.

Bannon, whose worldliness had been so crucial in Hearts' exhilarating journey to the quarter-finals of the same competition the previous year, had in his days with Dundee United sampled a European Cup semi-final and two legs of a UEFA final. No one is more qualified to assess the importance of Europe.

'In our previous run in the competition, the players proved that they were rapid learners in the business of European football. It was vital that we earn the chance to take that a stage further,' he insisted. 'Over a decade at Dundee United I watched young players improve in both technique and ability to handle the big occasion largely through their participation in the three club competitions.

'European experience is even more important in these days when the Premier Division restricts the number of opponents. Playing against each other four times does breed familiarity in the domestic game, and the opportunity to face different opponents, with different approaches, is increasingly invaluable.'

The naming, too, of Craig Levein and Dave McPherson in the Scotland squad for the World Cup and their subsequent performances in Italy, was yet another sign from a long, hard season that the quality of player being produced at Tynecastle was ever on the upgrade. McPherson played in all three first stage matches against Costa Rica, Sweden and Brazil and, although Craig's contribution was limited, by injury, to the full 90 minutes against the Swedes in Scotland's only victory, his input was no less pleasing.

It is not too fanciful to suggest that, in terms of the future, they represented the major finds for the Scotland national set-up and it was a pity that their unselfish efforts were, to a degree, sullied by post-competition difficulties. Perhaps inexperience may have led them to leave the team's hotel ahead of the others on the final evening in Italy after games in other sections had made it clear

Safe hands too – Nicky Walker

that Scotland's tournament had ended. Suggestions later that their international futures were in jeopardy were an over-reaction, considering some of the things that took place during the earlier days of Scotland's stay. Happily, that is now behind both players and long international careers seem sure for both men.

But the last word on the 1989/90 season should belong to the manager, MacDonald, who, despite having paid £100,000 for Nicky Walker, in no way sees that as a sign that Henry Smith's tenure as first choice goalkeeper is over. 'Henry is improving with every season and, at 34, if he looks after his fitness there is no reason to suppose that he won't be around for many seasons to come,' he said.

And the player himself is convinced that the experienced Walker's arrival has provided a welcome challenge at the right time. 'It's like starting all over again . . . Nicky coming to Hearts has been the best thing that's happened to me,' he confirmed.

CHAPTER ELEVEN
Into the Nineties

FROM THE moment Wallace Mercer and the Hearts board approached the problem of replacing Alex MacDonald, there was only one man who he was interested in. Joe Jordan was that man, and the chairman was determined to get him. Soundings that he had taken from many people in football - including Kenny Dalglish and Alex Ferguson - had indicated that he would be the man, but there were suggestions that Mercer might not succeed.

It took just a couple of meetings with the former Scotland player to convince both men that they had a common interest in coming together. Mercer had seen the positive opinions of Jordan confirmed, and the Bristol City man had observed the ambition in the Hearts chairman that he considered a pre-condition.

'Hearts are a big club with potential and everyone at the club indicated that they were ambitious. I am too, and together I hope that we can take the club forward over the next few years,' said Jordan.

The new man had impressed Mercer during the World Cup in Italy when Jordan had acted as press liaison for the Scottish Football Association in a highly impressive way. Everyone in the Scottish contingent was taken with the ease with which he executed the task. Mercer has watched the influx of foreign players into the game in Scotland and wanted a new manager with enough experience to take on board the opportunities from further afield. With his playing experience in Italy, Jordan certainly fitted that aspect of the job description. His record at Bristol City gave encouragement to Hearts. In financial terms he had turned the club round, and in the process had guided the West Country team from the Third Division into the Second.

'The game of football is changing dramatically and we have to change with it or be left behind. We believe that we have the man

Welcome aboard – the chairman and Joe

who can rise to the new challenges that will present themselves in the Nineties,' said Mercer.

It is as a player that Hearts fans recall the Lanarkshire man who started his playing career with Morton and who recollected during his introductory press conference that his previous visit to Tynecastle had been in Morton's reserve side. But it was in his Scotland role that this observer has fond memories of Jordan the player. When Joe Jordan was in the Scotland team they had a chance, no matter what the opposition. It was as simple as that. In the World Cup of 1982, when Jock Stein brought him into the side for the final group match against Russia, after an unconvincing victory over New Zealand and the heavy defeat in Seville by Brazil, the transformation was dramatic. Joe scored in that match, and although Scotland were still eliminated from the competition, the urgency and spirit that his introduction produced allowed the team to return home with credibility intact.

That same steely determination is still apparent in Jordan the manager, although it takes on a different form. As a player he was in constant motion, on and off the ball, and his physical presence represented an awesome sight for defenders. In his managerial guise he is a very careful, considered talker, but there is no mistaking the definite tone in his words. He knows exactly what he

It's the fans' turn on day one

wants from his players, and those who survive will be the ones who deliver.

In his first few weeks in charge, the players, who had all grown up as professionals with Alex MacDonald and in many cases had formed a close personal link with the former manager, were markedly impressed. Dispensing a quiet, firm discipline at training, he has quickly won their respect, vital, if the Hearts players present and future are to continue making the progress that has seen them develop so far already.

Jordan is the way forward, and he has come to a club that during the Eighties has gained the stability and credibility within the game to make Tynecastle a workplace with the potential he was seeking. It has not always been that way.

The thread through the last decade that we have traced pinpoints ten years during which there were more dramatic changes at Hearts Football Club than in any other period during their 116-year history.

Life in Division One has been banished, seemingly forever, and from dealing in hundreds of pounds on occasion for players, the club has paid £750,000 on two occasions in the last couple of years. From being a team with only a spectator's interest in matters international, Hearts has been able, during the opening months of the season, to field a side containing eight full internationalists, including four who have experienced the thrill of performing at World Cup finals.

So, if there have been times when it has been necessary to hold your breath while the changes swept through the club, it is almost certain that another startling and innovative decade lies ahead.

Already, Hearts are preparing for the challenge by instituting several fundamental changes in the commercial side of the business with the final years of this century very much in mind. The success of *Back From The Brink,* the official club video which took an objective look at recent history, and several publications connected with the club, have persuaded chairman Wallace Mercer and his board to form a publishing company. That is distinct from the very vigorous commercial department, which has now under its wing a new restaurant capable of seating 80 people at any one time, in order to provide the best in corporate facilities in the future.

In Mercer's time the commercial side has blossomed and, indeed, many innovative moves in the early part of the Eighties which were considered radical at the time have now become an accepted part of the game in Scotland. However, the chairman's view of the next ten years makes clear that not even the current level of commercial activity can on its own satisfy the hunger for financial investment that the top teams will develop.

His view sees the modern game extending far outwith the normal geographical boundaries that have perhaps in the past been imposed too rigidly by the game's administrators and indeed the clubs themselves. He pinpoints, in particular, the influence that satellite television has already established on the sport on both sides of the Border, and the massive financial contribution it is making to the domestic game.

'The sponsorship by BSB of the Scottish League looking into the next few years is quite staggering, and this is just the beginning,' he explained. 'The air time which will now be available to compaines interested in, for instance, trackside advertising will be vastly increased. And there are many other ways where the hours of football on television will be harnessed. However, it looks to me that we are heading for a period where the increased revenue will be accrued to a large extent by the bigger clubs. There is no doubt that the rich will get richer, and the poor poorer.'

He cites the new stadium requirements from UEFA and FIFA which will oblige clubs competing in the European tournaments to have all-seated stadia. This means that the search for cash outwith the traditional routes will become even more frantic. And as we have already seen, during the Eighties the cost of bringing quality players to the Premier League has been escalated by the Rangers experience and other factors.

Continued Mercer, 'We have been exceptionally fortunate over the last few years in being able to attract players of international calibre, whilst at the same time bringing through others from within our ranks to achieve that level.

'Make no mistake about it, the cost of recruiting that calibre of individual will continue to rise, and the rate of increase will escalate. Freedom of contract has already contributed to that and, although the transfer fees themselves may stay at manageable levels, the personal deals that players will command will make many of the top men outwith the reach of the majority of clubs.'

There will, in his view, be new competitions to pay for all this with, inevitably, a British competition of some sort and additional European matches involved.

'In terms of a new European tournament it may be that moves already being discussed by UEFA can head off the possibility of a breakaway by the top clubs in the main western European countries,' he added. 'In the very near future, it is almost certain that the three European competitions that we are familiar with will be restructured in order that the clubs with the very highest financial outlay will be given additional fixtures.

'That may be achieved by reorganising the early rounds so that, on a seeded basis, qualification for the later stages would be achieved from small groups of clubs playing each other home and away, very much in the format that was once used in the Scottish League Cup.'

Much of this is not new, of course, for on several occasions during the later years of the Eighties reports of clandestine meetings between the top clubs in England and Scotland have circulated, although there is a possibility that a return to Europe by England's clubs may elongate the time scale involved in such moves.

However, Mercer has watched with interest the number of changes in venue that are now being required in the early rounds

Looking ahead with Derek Ferguson

of our domestic club competitions, which represents a clear indication that many of our football grounds are simply not going to measure up. Therefore, looking even further ahead, he feels a franchise system based along American Football lines will be introduced.

'We would seem to be heading for that almost inevitably, where entry into inter-country tournaments would first be preceded by attaining certain standards. These would involve the standard of stadia, the playing reputation of clubs based over a number of years, the levels of financial investment that have been made and the ability to cope comfortably with crowds and the transport that would bring them to matches,' he warned. 'At the moment, it seems that there would be four clubs in Scotland that could be involved in the three main centres of population, Glasgow, Edinburgh and Aberdeen.

'When this will all happen is very difficult to predict, but one thing is for certain – Hearts, and anyone else who wishes to be a part of this new international football scene, must start preparing now. This in some way was the motivation behind the recent bid to buy Edinburgh Hibernian Plc. In hindsight, it might have been done differently, but there is no doubt that Edinburgh will need a top club playing in a top stadium if it wishes to be competitive at the highest level in the future.

'Even domestically, it is bad news if Rangers and Celtic become too dominant. And in this sense one thing has changed. I believe that would be bad business for them as well. At the start of this season I am sure David Murray and some 25,000 Rangers fans enjoyed watching them defeat East Stirling 5-0 in their first competitive match of the season. But when we are required to charge ever-increasing admission for games, how long would they be happy watching that?'

The arguments against such developments in the future are very similar to those raised when the Premier Division clubs threatened to break away from the Scottish League, before a compromise was eventually reached.

'Any similar venture could see clubs and players lose their affiliation to the world's top football bodies, and that is something that may never be resolved. However, it is difficult to see many of these radical changes being stopped,' admitted Mercer. 'There is big money in Europe now. More and more company ownership of the top football clubs on the Continent is becoming the norm, and that too could become a feature of the British game although development of that trend here is taking time to happen. Just look at Bernard Tapin, who owns Marseilles in France. Multi-million-pound transfers are commonplace at that club, and he has just purchased Adidas, the sportswear company. That is the calibre of businessman that is now involved.'

Big company connections through sponsorship have been a factor in Scottish football for many years and it may be that the Hearts chairman's scenario for the future will establish itself by way of an extension to the main sponsors' theme.

How long will it take for one of the multinational companies who already spend, in some cases, millions of pounds simply as a promotional or marketing exercise, to take their investment one stage further? There is a very sound economic argument for suggesting that, having taken the sponsorship idea to its ultimate limit, another financial nudge along the way could buy control of many of the clubs in question.

And Mercer foresees a time when even at Tynecastle he may be forced to choose between retaining full control and stunting Hearts' growth, or taking on board a major partner in order to elevate his club among Europe's élite.

He explained, 'Although I have personal wealth, I cannot foresee a time when one individual can inject the kind of money that will be required to compete on a grand European scale. I have had tremendous pleasure from a decade's involvement with Hearts and it's been a privilege to be chairman of such a great club. But at the end of the day, when the time comes to admit there are bigger cash influxes necessary to take the club a vital stage forward, then I would not stand in the way of that progress.

'When that would happen, or who might be involved, is anybody's guess but again it is something that the club must prepare for and be ready to accept if the circumstances present themselves. It would be selfish of me to stand in the way of Hearts' going forward but I would insist on staying involved with the club. It has become such an important part of my life that I would need to retain an input.

'It does not seem that this has been taken on board yet by big companies in this country, but I would be surprised if a precedent is not forthcoming during the course of the next ten years.'

Mercer is, of course, part of a new generation of football club owners, and there is no doubt that the rules over the last few years have dramatically changed so that, however long he and his contemporaries stay in control, increasingly the day of the one man band is over.

A look back through the ten years just ended indicates just how powerful an influence the successful businessmen who have become involved have had in terms of how the typical football

Travel trappings for Craig Levein, Dave McPherson, Davie Kirkwood,
Nicky Walker, Alan McLaren, David McCreery and Scott Crabbe

spectator has changed. The introduction of family areas, where
Hearts was a forerunner in Scotland, and the vastly increasing
number of women who are attending games have been very
positive factors which have also changed the nature of the
companies who are now interested in forming a football connection.

'We have been lucky in Scotland in that the behaviour of fans
over the last few years has been exemplary. That in itself has
allowed us to concentrate on attracting new sections of the
community to the sport,' he said.

'We at Tynecastle have noticed that a whole new breed of
company are now happy to have a high profile involvement with
football, who previously spent their money in other areas because
of the bad publicity so closely connected with the game.

'The legislation which was introduced in 1981 was a tremendous
launch pad for cleaning up our act. In England they are now
catching up but even recently Queen's Park Rangers lost the
Dutch airline, KLM, as their main sponsor. That should act as a
reminder that the consequences of letting our guard slip in
Scotland can be a heavy financial penalty in more ways than
one.

'If this welcome trend continues then it is surely inevitable that business and industry will increasingly see football as an acceptable vehicle for international promotion and, at more local level, a route by which they can directly access customers on an individual basis.'

Exactly where Hearts will be playing during the course of these changes taking shape was placed in doubt during the course of 1990, when plans to move from Tynecastle to the west side of the city were outlined. It seems clear that a move from the city centre is inevitable, although the circumstances of such a step are still clouded.

Reflected Mercer, 'We're caught in the middle of two ideals to some extent, after the tragedies at the Heysel Stadium and Hillsborough, which feature among the blackest ever days for football. The recent Taylor report into the loss of life at Sheffield and the Government's view of it on the one hand makes it essential that our stadia are upgraded to make certain that a repeat never ever happens. As a club we are totally committed to this and welcome the recent extension which allows us the period to the end of the century in which to provide all-seated accommodation with the necessary access and egress to ensure that our football stadium is exemplary.

'But, on the other hand, the cost of land in some of the areas on the city outskirts which would be suitable takes them outwith our reach. There is no way that we can finance a scheme where between £10 million and £20 million for a site is being asked. We simply cannot afford that. Politicians will have to make up their minds exactly what they want. We cannot in one instance be forced to provide such accommodation without the assistance of the community.

'But we are determined to see this through whatever the obstructions, and that is why the decision to move from Tynecastle has already been taken. We could have upgraded the ground to a perfectly acceptable standard, but we would forever be plagued with the problem of bad access. Therefore, to commit millions of pounds to refurbishing our present home without solving problems that can only get worse was not an acceptable option.'

League reconstruction is a subject that is rarely off the back pages for any length of time, and the last year has been no exception. However, Mercer is adamant that the structure which

Heading for a new era – Wallace Mercer

was achieved throughout the protracted breakaway movement should not be tampered with. He has even gone so far as to say that he would quit as chairman of Hearts should the demands for a 16-team top league in Scotland prove to be successful. And he explained that this should not be dismissed as either a bargaining ploy or a fit of pique from someone unable to get his own way. Financial viability is his motive.

'If the standard of our top clubs is to be maintained and improve, which is surely in the best interests of everyone, then the status quo must be protected,' he insisted. 'Even the critics of the Premier Division, set up within its ten-club structure, freely admit that all the obvious alternatives contain no substitutes for the successful aspects of the reconstruction that was fashioned in the Eighties.

'How can clubs like ourselves contemplate exchanging fixtures against Rangers, Celtic and Aberdeen for matches against clubs from the First Division? I mean no disrespect to these clubs, and applaud the considerable ambition that is being shown by many of them, but the financial consequences for the top clubs could be horrendous.

'Internationally, too, I believe that the Premier Division helps produce players more able to reach that standard. How could it help the national team to have the members of the squad playing one third of their games in one-sided, poorly attended fixtures?'

So the changes ahead from the boardroom's point of view are likely to be exciting and stimulating, and those thoughts make it interesting to look ahead into the 21st century and speculate what shape club football in Scotland could take.

Of course, managers and players will not only be involved in this evolution, but will, it is certain, be a part of the changes themselves.

One player at Tynecastle who has seen more of the world than most is midfield player Eamonn Bannon, who sees a massive revolution ahead for his playing colleagues. Bannon sees the potential for the best players as virtually limitless.

'Satellite television and real freedom of contract will produce earning potentials for players undreamt of before,' he suggested. 'Players will become European jetsetters, with a lifestyle in some cases similar to that of pop stars, golfers and tennis players. To say some will become multi-millionaires is not too fanciful. Sure, there have been individuals who have made vast sums but their numbers were few and that will broaden out considerably, in my opinion. At the moment we do not have complete freedom of contract, and that is soon to change. Players are not free of contract, they simply come to the end of their stipulated agreement.'

And he admits that the personal wealth that the football stars of the future will possess will polarise players even more pointedly in the future. Like Mercer's prognosis for clubs, Bannon reckons the top men will amass vast sums for their labours, while the gap between them and the less talented will continue to grow. 'Perhaps it is not justified morally, but big money will dictate in the end. It may be élitist, but that's what the fans nowadays want,' he added.

It is difficult to gauge what the paying customers in Scotland's top football stadia will be watching at the end of the Nineties, but it looks certain that the domestic discussions currently in vogue may soon appear trifling matters. The shape of our own leagues, and the numbers that are contained within them, may be of no consequence when set beside the wider international possibilities that lie ahead.

Broadfields
BISTRO BAR

Dear Customer,

We at Broadfields are one of the best bistro bar and restaurants on Edinburgh's east side and are pleased to offer you a wide and varied selection of superior quality food freshly prepared and served with care.

Patisserie available.

Club sandwiches and free coffee are served all day in the Lounge Bar.

Special 3 course lunches available for £3.25 per head.

Most credit cards and luncheon vouchers accepted.

Any queries please do not hesitate to call 031-657 4431 day or night.

Opening hours are as follows:—

	Lounge Bar
Mon-Sat	11.00 a.m.-12.00 p.m.
Sun	12.30 a.m.- 2.30 p.m.
	6.30 p.m.-11.00 p.m.
	Bistro
Mon-Sat	12.00 p.m.- 2.30 p.m.
	6.30 p.m until late
Sun	closed

96 Northfield Broadway   Edinburgh   EH8 7RU   031-657 4431

Mr. V's

Since Vito Crolla opened his first restaurant at Tollcross in 1972, his name has become a byword for 'La Cucina classica Italiana', but always with that special touch of the unusual.

Mr V's is the latest and finest example of his thoughtful and creative approach to Italian food which has attracted the patronage of local and international celebrities alike.

Tucked away in quiet Charlotte Lane, just seconds from the city centre, Mr V's offers a warm and friendly atmosphere unique with its tranquil, laburnum-filled courtyard. Its intimate, south-facing bar offers the perfect lead-in to the comfortable and elegant main restaurant above.

Seafood is a house speciality but there is also a tempting selection of meat, game and pasta dishes to choose from, each prepared with the consistent attention to high quality for which Vito Crolla is famed. A carefully chosen wine list compliments the varied and original dishes.

Vito Crolla's attention to personal service for all his customers ensures that, from the moment you arrive, you feel welcome and relaxed.

Head Chef, Filippo Librizi and his assistants have drawn together the best of Italian regional cuisine to offer you a mouth-watering and memorable gastronomic experience which you will look forward to enjoying time and again.

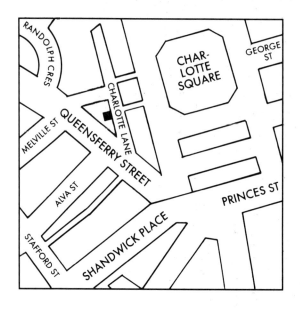

7 Charlotte Lane
Edinburgh
Tel: 031 220 0176

STATISTICS
PREMIER DIVISION CHAMPIONSHIP
SEASON 1980/81

	P	W	L	D	F	A	Pts.
CELTIC	36	26	6	4	84	37	56
ABERDEEN	36	19	6	11	61	26	49
RANGERS	36	16	8	12	60	32	44
ST MIRREN	36	18	10	8	56	47	44
DUNDEE UNITED	36	17	10	9	66	42	43
PARTICK THISTLE	36	10	16	10	32	48	30
AIRDRIEONIANS	36	10	17	9	36	55	29
MORTON	36	10	18	8	36	58	28
KILMARNOCK	36	5	22	9	23	65	19
HEART OF MIDLOTHIAN	36	6	24	6	27	71	18

FIRST DIVISION CHAMPIONSHIP
SEASON 1981/82

	P	W	L	D	F	A	Pts.
MOTHERWELL	39	26	4	9	92	36	61
KILMARNOCK	39	17	5	17	60	29	51
HEART OF MIDLOTHIAN	39	21	10	8	65	37	50
CLYDEBANK	39	19	12	8	61	53	46
ST JOHNSTONE	39	17	14	8	69	60	42
AYR UNITED	39	15	12	12	56	50	42
HAMILTON ACADEMICALS	39	16	15	8	52	49	40
QUEEN'S PARK	39	13	16	10	41	41	36
FALKIRK	39	11	14	14	49	52	36
DUNFERMLINE ATHLETIC	39	11	14	14	46	56	36
DUMBARTON	39	13	17	9	49	61	35
RAITH ROVERS	39	11	21	7	31	59	29
EAST STIRLINGSHIRE	39	7	22	10	38	77	24
QUEEN OF THE SOUTH	39	4	25	10	44	93	18

FIRST DIVISION CHAMPIONSHIP
SEASON 1982/83

	P	W	L	D	F	A	Pts.
ST JOHNSTONE	39	25	9	5	59	37	55
HEART OF MIDLOTHIAN	39	22	7	10	79	38	54
CLYDEBANK	39	20	9	10	72	49	50
PARTICK THISTLE	39	20	10	9	66	45	49
AIRDRIEONIANS	39	16	16	7	62	46	39
ALLOA	39	14	14	11	52	52	39
DUMBARTON	39	13	16	10	50	59	36
FALKIRK	39	15	18	6	45	55	36
RAITH ROVERS	39	13	18	8	64	63	34
CLYDE	39	14	19	6	55	66	34
HAMILTON ACADEMICALS	39	11	16	12	54	66	34
AYR UNITED	39	12	19	8	45	61	32
DUNFERMLINE ATHLETIC	39	7	15	17	39	69	31
QUEEN'S PARK	39	6	22	11	44	80	23

PREMIER DIVISION CHAMPIONSHIP
SEASON 1983/84

	P	W	L	D	F	A	Pts.
ABERDEEN	36	25	4	7	78	21	57
CELTIC	36	21	7	8	80	41	50
DUNDEE UNITED	36	18	7	11	67	39	47
RANGERS	36	15	9	12	53	41	42
HEART OF MIDLOTHIAN	36	10	10	16	38	47	36
ST MIRREN	36	9	13	14	55	59	32
HIBERNIAN	36	12	17	7	45	55	31
DUNDEE	36	11	20	5	50	74	27
ST JOHNSTONE	36	10	23	3	36	81	23
MOTHERWELL	36	4	25	7	31	75	15

PREMIER DIVISION CHAMPIONSHIP
SEASON 1984/85

	P	W	L	D	F	A	Pts.
ABERDEEN	36	27	4	5	89	26	59
CELTIC	36	22	6	8	77	30	52
DUNDEE UNITED	36	20	9	7	67	33	47
RANGERS	36	13	11	12	47	38	38
ST MIRREN	36	17	15	4	51	56	38
DUNDEE	36	15	14	7	48	50	37
HEART OF MIDLOTHIAN	36	13	18	5	47	64	31
HIBERNIAN	36	10	19	7	38	61	27
DUMBARTON	36	6	23	7	29	64	19
MORTON	36	5	29	2	29	100	12

PREMIER DIVISION CHAMPIONSHIP
SEASON 1985/86

	P	W	L	D	F	A	Pts.
CELTIC	36	20	6	10	67	38	50
HEART OF MIDLOTHIAN	36	20	6	10	59	33	50
DUNDEE UNITED	36	18	7	11	59	31	47
ABERDEEN	36	16	8	12	62	31	44
RANGERS	36	13	14	9	53	45	35
DUNDEE	36	14	15	7	45	51	35
ST MIRREN	36	13	18	5	42	63	31
HIBERNIAN	36	11	19	6	49	63	28
MOTHERWELL	36	7	23	6	33	66	20
CLYDEBANK	36	6	22	8	29	77	20

PREMIER DIVISION CHAMPIONSHIP
SEASON 1986/87

	P	W	L	D	F	A	Pts.
RANGERS	44	31	6	7	85	23	69
CELTIC	44	27	8	9	90	41	63
DUNDEE UNITED	44	24	8	12	66	36	60
ABERDEEN	44	21	7	16	63	29	58
HEART OF MIDLOTHIAN	44	21	9	14	64	43	56
DUNDEE	44	18	14	12	74	57	48
ST MIRREN	44	12	20	12	36	51	36
MOTHERWELL	44	11	21	12	43	64	34
HIBERNIAN	44	10	21	13	44	70	33
FALKIRK	44	8	26	10	31	70	26
CLYDEBANK	44	6	26	12	35	93	24
HAMILTON ACADEMICALS	44	6	29	9	39	93	21

PREMIER DIVISION CHAMPIONSHIP
SEASON 1987/88

	P	W	L	D	F	A	Pts.
CELTIC	44	31	3	10	79	23	72
HEART OF MIDLOTHIAN	44	23	5	16	74	32	62
RANGERS	44	26	10	8	85	34	60
ABERDEEN	44	21	6	17	56	25	59
DUNDEE UNITED	44	16	13	15	54	47	47
IIIBERNIAN	44	12	13	19	41	42	43
DUNDEE	44	17	20	7	70	64	41
MOTHERWELL	44	13	21	10	37	56	36
ST. MIRREN	44	10	19	15	41	64	35
FALKIRK	44	10	23	11	41	75	31
DUNFERMLINE ATHLETIC	44	8	26	10	41	84	26
MORTON	44	3	31	10	27	100	16

PREMIER DIVISION CHAMPIONSHIP
SEASON 1988/89

	P	W	L	D	F	A	Pts.
RANGERS	36	26	6	4	62	26	56
ABERDEEN	36	18	4	14	51	25	50
CELTIC	36	21	11	4	66	44	46
DUNDEE UNITED	36	16	8	12	44	26	44

HIBERNIAN	36	13	14	9	37	36	35
HEART OF MIDLOTHIAN	36	9	14	13	35	42	31
ST MIRREN	36	11	18	7	39	55	29
DUNDEE	36	9	17	10	34	48	28
MOTHERWELL	36	7	16	13	35	44	27
HAMILTON ACADEMICALS	36	6	28	2	19	76	14

PREMIER DIVISION CHAMPIONSHIP
SEASON 1989/90

	P	W	L	D	F	A	Pts.
RANGERS	36	20	5	11	48	19	51
ABERDEEN	36	17	9	10	56	33	44
HEART OF MIDLOTHIAN	36	16	8	12	54	35	44
DUNDEE UNITED	36	11	12	13	36	39	35
CELTIC	36	10	12	14	37	37	34
MOTHERWELL	36	11	13	12	43	47	34
HIBERNIAN	36	12	14	10	34	41	34
DUNFERMLINE ATHLETIC	36	11	17	8	37	50	30
ST MIRREN	36	10	16	10	28	48	30
DUNDEE	36	5	17	14	41	65	24

GOAL SCORERS (COMPETITIVE) 1980/81

	L	LC	SFAC	ASC	TOT
Chris Robertson		5		1	6
Frank Liddell	2				2
Walter Kidd	1				1
Alex Hamill	1				1
David Bowman	1	1			2
Scott Maxwell	1				1
Alfie Conn	3				3
Willie Gibson	4				4
Derek O'Connor	4			2	6
Pat McShane	1				1
Gary Liddell	2				2
Paul O'Brien	2				2
Alex MacDonald	3	1	1		5
Cammy Fraser	1				1
OG	1				1
	27	7	1	3	38

MAJOR SIGNINGS

Player	From	Date
Gary Mackay	Salvesen	
David Bowman	Salvesen	Summer 1980
Ian Westwater		
Stuart Gauld		
Chris Robertson	Rangers	May 1980
Alex MacDonald	Rangers	Aug. 1980
Peter Shields	Ipswich Town	Sept. 1980
Alfie Conn Jun	Pittsburg Spirit	July 1980
Paul O'Brien	Dundee United	Feb. 1980
Alex Hamill	Tottenham	Nov. 1980
John Robertson	Edina Hibs	Jan. 1981
Gary Liddell	Grimsby Town	Feb. 1981

TRANSFERS

Graham Shaw	Arbroath	May 1980
Crawford Boyd	Q.O.S.	Feb. 1981
Alfie Conn	Blackpool	March 1981
Jim Docherty	St Johnstone	Sept. 1980
Cammy Fraser	Dundee	Sept. 1980
Malcolm Robertson		Jan. 1981
Frees: Jim Denny, Archie White, Bobby Robinson,		May 1981

GOAL SCORERS (COMPETITIVE) 1981/82

	L	LC	SFAC	TOT
Willie Pettigrew	16			16
Gerry McCoy	9	1		10
Chris Robertson	7	2	1	10
Pat Byrne	8		1	9
Roddy MacDonald	6		1	7
Derek Addison	4			4
Derek O'Connor	4			4
Gary Liddell	2	2		4
Peter Marinello	2		1	3
Gary Mackay	2			2
Alex Hamill	2			2
Alex MacDonald	1			1
David Bowman	1			1
Peter Shields	1			1
	65	5	4	74

MAJOR SIGNINGS

Player	From	Date
Derek Strickland	Leicester City	July 1981
Pat Byrne	Leicester City	July 1981
Roddy MacDonald	Celtic	July 1981
Stewart MacLaren	Dundee	July 1981
Gerry McCoy	Queen's Park	July 1981
Henry Smith	Leeds United	July 1981
Brian McNeil	Plymouth	Aug. 1981
Willie Pettigrew	Dundee United	Sept. 1981
Derek Addison	Dundee United	Sept. 1981
Peter Marinello	Pheonix Inferno	Oct. 1981

TRANSFERS

Willie Gibson	Partick Thistle	July 1981
Jim Jefferies	Berwick	Nov. 1981
Paul O'Brien	St Johnstone	Nov. 1981
Frank Liddell	Free	Feb. 1982
Gary Liddell	Doncaster	March 1982
Colin More	Free	May 1981
Alex Hamill	Free	May 1981
Scott Maxwell	Free	June 1982
Brian McNeil	Free	June 1982
Derek Addison	St Johnstone	June 1982

GOAL SCORERS (COMPETITIVE) 1982/83

	L	LC	SFAC	TOT
Derek O'Connor	16	4	2	22
John Robertson	21			21
Willie Pettigrew	10	7		17
Alex MacDonald	5	3	1	9
David Bowman	5	2		7
Gary Mackay	6			6
Willie Johnston	6			6
Roddy MacDonald	3		1	4
Pat Byrne	3			3
Peter Shields		2	1	3
Sandy Jardine	2			2
Peter Marinello	1	1		2
OG	1	1		2
	79	20	5	104

MAJOR SIGNINGS

Player	From	Date
Sandy Jardine	Rangers	July 1982
Willie Johnston	Vancouver Whitecaps	Sep. 1982
Donald Park	Partick Thistle	May 1983
Malcolm Murray	Buckie Thistle	March 1983

TRANSFERS

Peter Marinello	Free	March 1983
Chris Robertson	Free	March 1983

GOAL SCORERS (COMPETITIVE) 1983/84

	L	LC	SFA	TOT
John Robertson	15	4	1	20
Jimmy Bone	7	1	1	9
Gary Mackay	4	2		6
Donald Park	4	1		5
Willie Johnston	2	1		3
George Cowie	1		1	2
Roddy MacDonald	2			2
Derek O'Connor	1	1		2
Alex MacDonald	1			1
Walter Kidd	1			1
	38	10	3	51

MAJOR SIGNINGS

Player	From	Date
Jimmy Bone	Hong Kong	Aug. 1983
Jimmy Sandison	Edin Emmettt	Aug. 1983
Craig Levein	Cowdenbeath	Nov. 1983
Gregor Stevens	(2 months loan)	Jan. 1984
Brian Whittaker	Celtic	May 1984
Kenny Black	Motherwell	June 1984
Brian McNaughton	Broxburn	June 1984

TRANSFERS

Pat Byrne	Shamrock Rovers	Sept. 1983
John Brough	Partick Thistle	Dec. 1983
Willie Pettigrew	Morton	Jan. 1984
Peter Shields	Free	May 1984
Gerry McCoy	Partick Thistle	March 1984

GOAL SCORERS (COMPETITIVE) 1984/85

	L	LC	SFAC	UEFA	TOT
John Robertson	8	1	2	2	13
Sandy Clark	8		1		9
Kenny Black	7				7
Gary Mackay	2		4		6
Jimmy Bone	4	1			5
Donald Park	3	1			4
Roddy MacDonald	1	1	1		3
Andy Watson	3				3
Brian McNaughton	2		1		3
Brian Whittaker	1	1			2
Craig Levein	1	1			2
Alex MacDonald	2				2
Derek O'Connor	1	1			2
Willie Johnston	1	1			2
Walter Kidd	1				1
David Bowman	1				1
OG	1				1
	47	8	9	2	66

MAJOR SIGNINGS

Player	From	Date
Sandy Clark	Rangers	Oct. 1984
Neil Berry	Bolton	Dec. 1984
Andy Watson	Leeds	Dec. 1984
Ian Jardine	Anthorsis Cyprus	May 1985
John Colquhoun	Celtic	May 1985

TRANSFERS

David Bowman	Coventry	Dec. 1984
Derek O'Connor	Free	Jan. 1985
Willie Johnston	Free	March 1985
Jimmy Bone	Arbroath	Feb. 1985
Stewart MacLaren	Free	May 1985

GOAL SCORERS (COMPETITIVE) 1985/86

	L	LC	SFAC	TOT
John Robertson	20	1	4	25
Sandy Clark	12			12
John Colquhoun	8	1	2	11
Ian Jardine	7			7
Gary Mackay	4		2	6
Kenny Black	2		1	3
Neil Berry	2			2
Roddy MacDonald	2			2
Craig Levein	2			2
Walter Kidd		1		1
Brian McNaughton		1		1
Paul Cherry		1		1
Colin McAdam			1	1
	59	5	10	74

MAJOR SIGNINGS

Player	From	Date
Scott Crabbe	Tynecastle BC	July 1985
Colin McAdam	Adelaide City	Sep. 1985
Billy Mackay	Rangers	Feb. 1986

TRANSFERS

Donald Park	Brechin	July 1985
Brian McNaughton	East Fife	June 1986

GOAL SCORERS (COMPETITIVE) 1986/87

	L	LC	SFAC	UEFA	TOT
John Robertson	16		2	1	19
John Colquhoun	13		1		14
Sandy Clark	8			1	9
Gary Mackay	7		2		9
Roddy MacDonald	5				5
Wayne Foster	4		2	1	7
Neil Berry	3				3
Andy Watson	3				3
Kenny Black	1		1		2
Sandy Jardine	1				1
Ian Jardine	1				1
George Cowie	1				1
OG	1				1
	64		8	3	75

Player	From	Date
Wayne Foster	P.N.E.	Aug. 1986
Allan Moore	Dumbarton	Nov. 1986

TRANSFERS

Willie Irvine	Free	Sept. 1986
Colin McAdam	Partick Thistle	Oct. 1986
Paul Cherry	Cowdenbeath	Aug. 1986

GOAL SCORERS (COMPETITIVE) 1987/88

	L	LC	SFAC	TOT
John Robertson	26	3	2	31
John Colquhoun	15		1	16
Sandy Clark	6	2	1	9
Gary Mackay	5	1	2	8
Wayne Foster	4	1	2	7
Mike Galloway	6			6
Dave McPherson	4	1		5
Kenny Black	4			4
Ian Jardine	2			2
Neil Berry		1		1
Allan Moore	1			1
Brian Whittaker			1	1
OG	1			1
	74	9	9	92

MAJOR SIGNINGS

Player	From	Date
Dave McPherson	Rangers	July 1987
Hugh Burns	Rangers	July 1987
Mike Galloway	Halifax	Nov. 1987
Martin Christie	Hutcheson Vale	Dec. 1987
Mark Gavin	Rochdale	Jan. 1988
Eammon Bannon	Dundee United	June 1988

TRANSFERS

Andy Watson	Hibs	Aug. 1987
Billy Mackay	Retired (knee injury)	Aug. 1987
Roddy McDonald	Morton	Sept. 1987
John Robertson	Newcastle	April 1988

GOAL SCORERS (COMPETITIVE) 1988/89

	L	LC	SFAC	UEFA	TOT
Iain Ferguson	5	5		1	11
Mike Galloway	2		1	5	8
John Colquhoun	5	1	2	1	9
Gary Mackay	2	2			4
Sandy Clark	1				1
Dave McPherson	4		1		5
Eamonn Bannon	2		2	1	5
Kenny Black	1	1		1	3
John Robertson	4				4
Wayne Foster	1			1	2
Ian Jardine	1	1			2
Allan Moore	2				2
Alan McLaren	1				1

Tom McKinlay	1				1
Neil Berry	1				1
Malcolm Murray		1			1
OG	2		1		3
	35	11	7	10	63

MAJOR SIGNINGS

Player	From	Date
Iain Ferguson	Dundee United	July 1988
Murray McDermott	(4 months contract)	Aug. 1988
Tom McKinlay	Dundee	Dec. 1988
John Robertson	Newcastle United	Dec. 1988
Peter McCoy	Unattached (Coach)	Dec. 1988

TRANSFERS

Andy Bruce	Free to join police	Aug. 1988
Mark Gavin	Bristol City	Sept. 1988
Hugh Burns	Dunfermline	Dec. 1988
Malcolm Murray	Hull City	April 1989
Kenny Black	Portsmouth (£280,000)	May 1989
Allan Moore	St Johnstone (£85,000)	May 1989
Mike Galloway	Celtic (£550,000)	June 1989

GOAL SCORERS (COMPETITIVE) 1989/90

	L	LC	SFAC	TOT
John Robertson	17	1	4	22
Scott Crabbe	12	4	1	17
John Colquhoun	6		2	8
Husref Musemic	3	1		4
Dave McPherson	4			4
Iain Ferguson	1			1
Eamonn Bannon	2	1		3
Jimmy Sandison	2			2
Walter Kidd	1	1		2
Neil Berry	1			1
Gary Mackay	1			1
David Kirkwood		1		1
Wayne Foster	1			1
Tom McKinlay	1			1
Alan McLaren	1			1
OG	1			1
	54	9	7	70

MAJOR SIGNINGS

Player	From	Date
Husref Musemic	Red Star Belgrade	June 1989
Nicky Walker	Rangers	Aug. 1989
David Kirkwood	Rangers	July 1989
David McCreery	Sudsvall	Sept. 1989
Sandy Clark	Dunfermline	April 1990

TRANSFERS

Sandy Clark	Partick Thistle	Nov. 1989
Ian Jardine	Partick Thistle	Dec. 1989
Husref Musemic	Sarajevo	Jan 1990
Iain Ferguson	Charlton	Loan Contract
Iain Ferguson	Bristol City	Loan Contract

PREMIER DIVISION CHAMPIONSHIP
SEASON 1980/81

Date	Opponents	Comp	Venue	F	A	Scorer
July 25	Chelsea	F	H	0	1	
July 30	Airdrieonians	S	A	0	3	
Aug. 2	Glenavon	F	A	3	3	O'Connor, C. Robertson, OG
Aug. 4	Newcastle	F	H	1	1	C. Robertson
Aug. 6	Airdrieonians	S	H	3	3	C. Robertson, O'Connor 2
Aug. 9	Partick Th.	PL	A	2	3	Liddell, Fraser, P
Aug. 13	Berwick Rangers	ESS	H	0	0	
Aug. 16	Airdrieonians	PL	H	0	2	
Aug. 20	Hibernian	ESS	H	2	2	Gibson 2
Aug. 23	St Mirren	PL	A	3	1	Conn, O'Connor 2
Aug. 27	Montrose	LC	H	2	1	C. Robertson, A. MacDonald
Aug. 30	Montrose	LC	A	3	1	C. Robertson 3
Sept. 3	Ayr United	LC	H	2	3	C. Robertson, Bowman
Sept. 6	Kilmarnock	PL	A	1	0	Gibson
Sept. 13	Celtic	PL	H	0	2	
Sept. 20	Morton	PL	H	0	1	
Sept. 24	Ayr United	LC	A	0	4	
Sept. 27	Dundee United	PL	A	1	1	O'Connor
Oct. 4	Aberdeen	PL	H	0	1	
Oct. 11	Rangers	PL	A	1	3	MacDonald
Oct. 18	Partick Th.	PL	H	0	1	
Oct. 25	Airdrieonians	PL	A	0	3	
Nov. 1	St Mirren	PL	H	1	1	Conn
Nov. 8	Dundee United	PL	H	0	3	
Nov. 15	Morton	PL	A	2	2	Conn, O'Connor
Nov. 22	Rangers	PL	H	0	0	
Dec. 6	Kilmarnock	PL	H	2	0	MacDonald, O'Brien
Dec. 13	Celtic	PL	A	2	3	MacDonald, Gibson
Dec. 20	Morton	PL	H	0	0	
Dec. 27	Dundee United	PL	A	1	4	Gibson
Jan. 1	Airdrieonians	PL	H	2	3	Gibson, O'Brien
Jan. 3	Partick Th.	PL	A	0	1	
Jan. 10	Aberdeen	PL	H	0	2	
Jan. 24	Morton	SC	A	0	0	
Jan. 28	Morton	SC	H	1	3	MacDonald
Jan. 31	Celtic	PL	H	0	3	
Feb. 16	Dunfermline	F	A	1	1	O'Brien
Feb. 21	St Mirren	PL	A	1	2	M'Shane
Feb. 28	Partick Th.	PL	H	1	1	Kidd
March 7	Aberdeen	PL	A	1	4	Hamill
March 14	Rangers	PL	H	2	1	OG, F. Liddell
March 21	Morton	PL	A	0	3	
March 24	Kilmarnock	PL	A	0	2	
March 29	Dundee United	PL	H	0	4	
April 1	Celtic	PL	A	0	6	
April 4	Kilmarnock	PL	A	1	0	Bowman
April 11	Aberdeen	PL	A	0	1	
April 18	St Mirren	PL	H	1	2	Maxwell
April 25	Airdrieonians	PL	A	2	1	G. Liddell 2
May 2	Rangers	PL	A	0	4	

PREMIER DIVISION CHAMPIONSHIP
SEASON 1981/82

Date	Opponents	Venue	Comp	F	A	Scorer
July 25	North Shields	A	F	4	2	McCoy 2, G. Liddell, Shields, P
July 27	Whitley Bay	A	F	1	1	Byrne
July 29	Blyth Spartans	A	F	3	1	McCoy, G. Liddell, O'Brien

Date	Opponent	H/A	Comp	F	A	Scorers
Aug. 1	Sunderland	H	F	0	1	
Aug. 8	Aidrie	A	LC	1	0	C. Robertson
Aug. 12	Aberdeen	H	LC	1	0	C. Robertson
Aug 15	Kilmarnock	H	LC	1	1	G. Liddell
Aug. 19	Aberdeen	A	LC	0	3	
Aug. 21	Dunfermline	A	D1	1	1	G. Liddell
Aug. 23	Airdrie	H	LC	2	3	McCoy, G. Liddell
Aug. 26	Kilmarnock	A	LC	0	2	
Sept. 5	Kilmarnock	H	D1	0	1	
Sept. 12	Falkirk	A	D1	0	0	
Sept. 16	Hamilton	H.	D1	2	1	Hamill, Mackay
Sept. 19	Clydebank	H	D1	1	0	O'Connor
Sept. 23	Ayr United	A	D1	0	0	
Sept. 26	Dumbarton	H	D1	2	1	R. McDonald, O'Connor
Oct. 3	Queen's Park	A	D1	0	1	
Oct. 7	St Johnstone	H	D1	3	1	O'Connor 2, Pettigrew
Oct. 10	Q.O.S.	A	D1	2	1	Shields, Addison
Oct. 17	Raith Rovers	H	D1	2	1	R. McDonald, G. Liddell
Oct. 24	Motherwell	A	D1	2	2	Pettigrew 2
Oct. 27	Hibernian	A	ESS	2	1	OG, R. McDonald
Oct. 31	East Stirling	H	D1	0	1	
Nov. 7	Kilmarnock	A	D1	0	0	
Nov. 14	Dunfermline	H	D1	1	1	C. Robertson
Nov. 21	Hamilton	A	D1	2	0	Mackay, Addison
Nov. 28	Dumbarton	A	D1	1	3	Marinello
Dec. 5	Queen's Park	H	D1	1	1	Pettigrew
Dec. 30	Aberdeen	A	F	1	2	C. Robertson
Jan. 20	Meadowbank	H	ESS	5	0	Pettigrew 4, Byrne
Jan. 27	East Stirling	A	SC	4	1	Byrne, R. McDonald, C. Robertson, Marinello
Jan. 30	Motherwell	H	D1	0	3	
Feb. 6	East Stirling	A	D1	1	0	Byrne
Feb. 9	Falkirk	H	D1	3	0	McCoy, Pettigrew, Marinello
Feb. 13	Forfar	H	SC	0	1	
Feb. 17	Q.O.S.	H	D1	4	1	R. McDonald, Pettigrew, McCoy, C. Robertson
Feb. 20	Ayr United	A	D1	3	0	Byrne, Petigrew, McCoy
Feb. 23	St Johnstone	A	D1	1	2	McCoy
Feb. 27	Raith Rovers	H	D1	4	0	Bowman, McCoy 2, C. Robertson
March 6	Falkirk	A	D1	1	3	C. Robertson
March 13	Q.O.S.	A	D1	5	1	Byrne, P, Pettigrew 3, Addison
March 20	Queen's Park	H	D1	1	0	Byrne
March 27	Clydebank	A	D1	1	2	Byrne, P
March 31	Raith Rovers	A	D1	3	0	R. McDonald, C. Robertson 2
April 3	St Johnstone	H	D1	3	0	R. McDonald, McCoy 2
April 10	Hamilton	A	D1	2	0	Pettigrew, A MacDonald
April 14	Clydebank	A	D1	5	1	Byrne, Pettigrew 4
April 21	Ayr United	H	D1	2	1	Hamill, Addison
April 24	Dunfermline	A	D1	2	1	R. McDonald, C. Robertson
May 1	Dumbarton	H	D1	2	5	Byrne, Pettigrew
May 8	Kilmarnock	A	D1	0	0	
May 15	Mother ell	H	D1	0	3	

PREMIER DIVISION CHAMPIONSHIP
SEASON 1982/83

Date	Opponents	Venue	Comp	F	A	Scorer
Aug. 4	Sheffield United	F	H	4	2	Kidd, Mackay 2, Bowman
Aug. 7	Leeds	H	F	1	0	OG
Aug. 9	Hibernian	A	F	0	1	
Aug. 14	Motherwell	A	LC	1	2	O'Connor
Aug. 18	Forfar	H	LC	2	1	O'Connor
Aug. 21	Clyde	A	LC	7	1	Pettigrew 4, Bowman, Shields, OG
Aug 25	Forfar	A	LC	2	0	A. MacDonald, Marinello
Aug. 28	Motherwell	H	LC	1	0	A. MacDonald
Sept. 1	Clyde	H	LC	3	0	Bowman, Shields, Pettigrew
Sept. 4	Queen's Park	A	D1	2	1	Marinello Bowman
Sept. 11	Ayr United	H	D1	1	1	O'Connor
Sept. 15	St Mirren	A	LC	1	1	Pettigrew
Sept. 18	Falkirk	A	D1	1	0	O'Connor
Sept. 22	St Mirren	H	D1	2	1	A. MacDonald, Pettigrew
Sept. 25	Clyde	H	D1	1	0	Bowman
Sept. 29	Clydebank	H	D1	4	1	Pettigrew, O'Connor, Byrne, Jardine
Oct. 2	Raith Rovers	A	D1	0	1	
Oct. 6	Dumbarton	H	D1	1	1	O'Connor
Oct. 9	Alloa	H	D1	3	0	OG, R. McDonald, Robertson
Oct. 16	Hamilton	A	D1	3	1	A. MacDonald, Byrne, O'Connor
Oct. 23	Dunfermline	H	D1	4	1	O'Connor, Bowman, Johnston, A.McDonald
Oct. 27	Rangers	A	LC	0	2	
Oct. 30	Partick Th.	A	D1	1	1	Robertson
Nov. 6	Airdrie	H	D1	2	4	O'Connor, Jardine, P
Nov. 10	Rangers	H	LC	1	2	O'Connor
Nov. 13	Clydebank	3	0	A	D1	Mackay, O'Connor, Robertson
Nov. 20	Falkirk	H	D1	3	1	Johnston, Robertson 2
Nov. 24	Dynamo Kiev	H	F	0	2	
Nov. 27	Dumbarton	A	D1	1	1	O'Connor
Dec. 4	Raith Rovers	H	D1	2	0	Mackay, Johnston, P
Dec. 11	Clyde	A	D1	3	2	A. MacDonald, Pettigrew
Dec. 27	Ayr United	A	D1	3	0	Pettigrew, O'Connor, A. MacDonald
Jan. 1	St Johnstone	H	D1	1	0	Pettigrew
Jan. 3	Airdrie	A	D1	1	0	Pettigrew
Jan. 8	Hamilton	H	D1	2	1	Pettigrew, O'Connor
Jan. 15	Alloa	A	D1	0	0	
Jan. 22	Partick Th.	H	D1	0	1	
Jan. 28	Q.O.S.	A	SC	1	1	Shields
Feb. 2	Q.O.S.	H	SC	1	0	O'Connor
Feb. 9	Dunfermline	A	D1	1	2	A. McDonald
Feb. 12	Ayr United	H	D1	5	1	O'Connor, Mackay, Pettigrew, Bowman, Byrne
Feb. 20	East Fife	H	SC	2	1	R. McDonald, O'Connor
Feb. 26	Queen's Park	A	D1	3	0	Robertson 3
March 5	Falkirk	H	D1	1	2	O'Connor
March 12	Celtic	A	SC	1	4	A.McDonald
March 19	Partick Th.	H	D1	4	0	Robertson 3, Pettigrew
March 26	Clyde	H	D1	3	1	Robertson, Mackay, R. McDonald
March 29	Raith Rovers	A	D1	2	4	Johnston 2, 1P
April 2	Airdrie	A	D1	2	0	Mackay, P, Robertson
April 6	Queen's Park	H	D1	2	0	Robertson, O'Connor
April 9	St Johnstone	A	D1	1	2	Bowman
April 16	Clydebank	H	D1	2	2	Robertson 2
April 23	Alloa	A	D1	1	1	A. MacDonald
April 30	Dunfermline	H	D1	3	3	Robertson, 3
May 7	Dumbarton	A	D1	4	0	Robertson 2, O'Connor, Mackay
May 14	Hamilton	H	D1	2	0	Johnston, O'Connor

FIXTURES, RESULTS, SCORERS 1983/84

Date	Opponents	Comp	Venue	F	A	Scorers
Aug. 1	Nairn County	F	A	8	0	Bowman 2, Mackay, A. MacDonald, Park 2, R. MacDonald 2
Aug. 3	Inverness Caley	F	A	0	2	
Aug. 6	Elgin City	F	A	1	0	Cowie
Aug. 9	Leeds United	F	H	0	0	
Aug. 13	Leicester City	F	H	2	3	Robertson 2
Aug. 20	St Johnstone	PL	A	1	0	Bone
Aug. 24	Cowdenbeath	LC	A	0	0	
Aug. 27	Cowdenbeath	LC	H	1	1	Mackay (won 4-2 on pens.)
Aug. 31	St Mirren	LC	A	2	2	Bone, Robertson, P
Sept. 3	Hibernian	PL	H	3	2	Robertson 2, Bone
Sept. 7	Rangers	LC	H	0	3	
Sept. 10	Rangers	PL	H	3	1	A. MacDonald, Robertson, Bone
Sept. 17	Dundee	PL	A	2	1	Bone, Robertson
Sept. 20	Berwick	ESS	H	0	2	
Sept. 24	St Mirren	PL	A	1	0	R. MacDonald
Oct. 1	Aberdeen	PL	H	0	2	
Oct. 5	Clydebank	LC	H	1	1	Park
Oct. 8	Motherwell	PL	H	0	0	
Oct. 15	Celtic	PL	A	1	1	Bone
Oct. 22	Dundee United	PL	A	0	1	
Oct. 26	Rangers	LC	A	0	2	
Oct. 29	St Johnstone	PL	H	2	0	Robertson 2, 1P
Nov. 5	Hibernian	PL	A	1	1	Robertson
Nov. 9	St Mirren	LC	H	3	1	O'Connor, Mackay, P, Robertson
Nov. 13	Dundee	PL	H	1	3	Mackay, P
Nov. 19	Aberdeen	PL	A	0	2	
Nov. 26	St Mirren	PL	H	2	2	Mackay 2, 1P
Nov. 30	Clydebank	LC	A	3	0	Robertson 2, Johnston
Dec. 3	Rangers	PL	A	0	3	
Dec. 10	Dundee United	PL	H	0	0	
Dec. 17	Celtic	PL	H	1	3	Robertson
Dec. 26	Motherwell	PL	A	1	1	Bone
Dec. 31	St Johnstone	PL	A	2	1	Park, Cowie
Jan. 2	Hibernian	PL	H	1	1	Park
Jan. 7	Dundee	PL	A	1	4	Robertson
Feb. 6	Partick Th.	SC	H	2	0	Cowie, Bone
Feb. 11	Rangers	PL	H	2	2	O'Connor, Robertson
Feb. 18	Dundee United	SC	A	1	2	Robertson, P
Feb. 25	Celtic	PL	A	1	4	Park
March 3	Motherwell	PL	H	2	1	Robertson 2
March 11	Dundee United	PL	A	1	3	Kidd
March 17	St Mirren	PL	A	1	1	Johnston
March 24	St Mirren	PL	H	2	1	Robertson, Bone
March 27	Berwick	ESS	A	0	3	
March 31	Dundee United	PL	H	0	0	
April 2	Aberdeen	PL	A	1	1	Robertson
April 7	Rangers	PL	A	0	0	
April 15	Arsenal	F	H	3	2	Kidd, Bone, Mackay
April 21	Hibernian	PL	A	0	0	
April 28	St Johnstone	PL	H	2	2	R. MacDonald, Park
May 2	Aberdeen	PL	H	0	1	
May 5	Celtic	PL	H	1	1	Johnston
May 9	Dundee	PL	H	1	1	Mackay
May 12	Motherwell	PL	A	1	0	Robertson, P
May 13	Buckie Th.	F	A	3	2	R. MacDonald, Park, Johnston
May 15	Rangers	F	H	2	3	Mackay, Robertson

FIXTURES, RESULTS, SCORERS 1984/85

Date	Opponents	Comp	Venue	F	A	Scorers
July 28	Ross County	F	A	2	2	Mackay 2
July 30	Wick Academy	F	A	7	1	O'Connor 3, Park, Black, P, Whittaker, A. MacDonald
Aug. 1	Inverness Clach	F	A	5	2	Bone, Robertson, Mackay, Black, P, R. MacDonald
Aug. 4	Elgin City	F	A	2	0	Levein, Black, P
Aug. 7	Queen's Park	F	H	3	2	R. MacDonald, Robertson, OG
Aug. 11	Dundee United	PL	A	0	2	
Aug. 18	Morton	PL	H	1	2	Whittaker
Aug. 22	E. Stirling	LC	H	4	0	Bone, Levein, Johnston, Whittaker
Aug. 25	Hibernian	PL	A	2	1	Levein, O'Connor;
Aug. 29	Ayr United	LC	H	1	0	O'Connor
Sept. 1	Dumbarton	PL	H	1	0	Park
Sept. 4	Dundee	LC	A	1	0	R. MacDonald
Sept. 8	St Mirren	PL	H	1	2	Robertson, P
Sept. 15	Celtic	PL	A	0	1	
Sept. 19	Paris St Germain	UEFA	A	0	4	
Sept. 22	Dundee	PL	H	0	2	
Sept. 26	Dundee United	LC	H	1	2	Robertson
Sept. 29	Aberdeen	PL	A	0	4	
Oct. 3	Paris St Germain	UEFA	H	2	2	Robertson 2
Oct. 6	Rangers	PL	H	1	0	Robertson
Oct. 10	Dundee United	PL	H	1	3	Park
Oct. 13	Dundee United	PL	H	2	0	Park, Robertson
Oct. 20	Morton	PL	A	3	2	Black, P, Robertson, Clark
Oct. 27	Hibernian	PL	H	0	0	
Nov. 3	Dumbarton	PL	A	1	0	Bone
Nov. 10	St Mirren	PL	A	3	2	Clark 2, Bone
Nov. 17	Celtic	PL	H	1	5	Johnston
Nov. 24	Dundee	PL	A	1	2	Bowman
Dec. 1	Aberdeen	PL	H	1	2	A. MacDonald
Dec. 8	Rangers	PL	A	1	1	Park
Dec. 15	Dundee United	PL	A	2	5	Black, P, Bone
Dec. 29	Morton	PL	H	1	0	Black, P
Jan. 1	Hibernian	PL	A	2	1	Mackay, Clark
Jan. 5	Dumbarton	PL	H	5	1	Black 3, 1P, Clark, Bone
Jan. 12	St Mirren	PL	H	0	1	
Jan. 30	Inverness Caley	SC	H	6	0	R. MacDonald, Mackay 4, Robertson
Feb. 3	Dundee	PL	H	3	3	Robertson, Mackay, McNaughton
Feb. 9	Aberdeen	PL	A	2	2	Watson, Robertson
Feb. 16	Brechin City	SC	A	1	1	Robertson
Feb. 20	Brechin City	SC	H	1	0	McNaughton
Feb. 23	Rangers	PL	H	2	0	Watson, R. MacDonald
March 2	Morton	PL	A	1	0	A. MacDonald
March 9	Aberdeen	SC	H	1	1	Clark
March 13	Aberdeen	SC	A	0	1	
March 16	Dundee United	PL	H	0	1	
March 20	Celtic	PL	A	2	3	Robertson, Watson
March 23	Dumbarton	PL	H	3	1	Kidd, Clark 2
April 2	Hibernian	PL	H	2	2	Robertson, Clark
April 6	Celtic	PL	H	0	2	
April 20	Dundee	PL	A	0	3	
April 24	Eintracht Frankfurt	F	H	3	1	Clark, McNaughton, Robertson
April 27	Rangers	PL	A	1	3	McNaughton
May 4	Aberdeen	PL	H	0	3	
May 11	St Mirren	PL	A	2	5	OG, Black

FIXTURES, RESULTS, SCORERS 1985/86

Date	Opponents	Venue	Comp	F	A	Scorers
July 25	Saarwellingen	A	F	2	0	OG, Watson
July 26	Wiesbaden	A	F	0	0	
July 29	Ingleheim	A	F	5	1	Black, R. McDonald, Watson, OG
Aug. 3	S.G. Eintracht	A	F	4	1	Robertson 2, Kidd, Mackay
Aug. 4	Birkenfeld	A	F	2	1	Mackay 2
Aug. 10	Celtic	H	PL	1	1	Colquhoun
Aug. 17	St Mirren	A	PL	2	6	Colquhoun, Robertson
Aug. 20	Montrose	A	SC	3	1	Kidd, Colquhoun, Robertson
Aug. 24	Rangers	A	PL	1	3	Robertson
Aug. 27	Stirling Albion	H	SC	2	1	McNaughton, Cherry
Aug. 31	Hibernian	H	PL	2	1	Colquhoun, Clark
Sept. 4	Aberdeen	A	SC	0	1	
Sept. 7	Aberdeen	A	PL	0	3	
Sept. 14	Dundee United	H	PL	2	0	R. McDonald, Robertson
Sept. 21	Motherwell	A	PL	1	2	I. Jardine
Sept. 28	Clydebank	A	PL	0	1	
Oct 5	Dundee	H	PL	1	1	I. Jardine
Oct 12	Celtic	A	PL	1	0	Robertson
Oct 19	St Mirren	H	PL	3	0	Mackay, Robertson 2
Oct 23	Arbroath	A	F	4	1	Clark, Mackay 2, Robertson
Oct 30	Aberdeen	H	PL	1	0	Levein
Nov. 2	Dundee United	A	PL	1	1	I. Jardine
Nov. 9	Hibernian	A	PL	0	0	
Nov. 16	Rangers	H	PL	3	0	Clark 2, Robertson
Nov. 23	Motherwell	H	PL	3	0	I. Jardine, Clark 2
Nov. 30	Clydebank	H	PL	4	1	Black, P, Berry, Clark, Robertson
Dec. 7	Dundee	A	PL	1	1	I. Jardine
Dec. 14	Celtic	H	PL	1	1	Robertson
Dec. 21	St Mirren	A	PL	1	0	Black
Dec. 28	Rangers	A	PL	2	0	Colquhoun 2
Jan. 1	Hibernian	H	PL	3	1	I. Jardine, Clark, Robertson
Jan. 4	Motherwell	A	PL	3	1	Berry, I. Jardine, Robertson
Jan. 11	Dundee United	H	PL	1	1	Mackay
Jan. 18	Aberdeen	A	PL	1	0	Colquhoun
Jan. 25	Rangers	H	SC	3	2	Mackay, Robertson, McAdam
Feb. 1	Clydebank	A	PL	1	1	Clark
Feb. 8	Dundee	H	PL	3	1	Colquhoun, Mackay, Robertson
Feb. 22	Celtic	A	PL	1	1	Robertson
March 3	Hamilton	A	SC	2	1	Mackay, Robertson
March 9	St Mirren	H	SC	4	1	Colquhoun, Black, Robertson 2, 1P
March 15	Motherwell	H	PL	2	0	R. McDonald, Robertson, P
March 22	Hibernian	A	PL	2	1	Clark, Robertson, P
March 25	St Mirren	H	PL	3	0	Levein, Clark, Robertson
March 29	Rangers	H	Pl	3	1	Clark, Robertson 2,1P
April 5	Dundee United	Hamp	SC	1	0	Colquhoun
April 12	Dundee United	A	PL	3	0	Clark, Robertson 2
April 20	Aberdeen	H	PL	1	1	Colquhoun
April 26	Clydebank	H	PL	1	0	Mackay
May 3	Dundee	A	PL	0	2	
May 6	Hibernian	A	ESS	2	1	Mackay. 1P
May 10	Aberdeen	Hamp	SC	0	3	

FIXTURES, RESULTS, SCORERS 1986/87

Date	Opponents	Comp	Venue	F	A	Scorer
July 28	Stoke City	F	A	0	1	
July 30	Wigan Athletic	F	A	1	1	Colquhoun
July 31	Bohemians	F	A	3	0	Colquhoun, Watson, W. Irvine
Aug. 5	Watford	F	H	2	1	Colquhoun, Clark
Aug. 9	St Mirren	PL	A	0	0	

Date	Opponents	Comp	Venue	F	A	Scorers
Aug. 13	Hamilton	PL	H	1	0	Robertson
Aug. 16	Falkirk	PL	H	1	0	Watson
Aug. 19	Montrose	SKC	H	0	2	
Aug. 23	Dundee United	PL	A	0	1	
Aug. 30	Hibernian	PL	A	3	1	I. Jardine, Clark, Robertson
Sept. 2	Manchester Utd	F	H	2	2	I. Jardine, Watson
Sept. 6	Clydebank	PL	H	2	1	G. Mackay, Foster
Sept. 13	Aberdeen	PL	A	1	0	Clark
Sept. 17	Dukla Prague	UEFA	H	3	2	Clark, Foster, Robertson
Sept. 20	Motherwell	PL	H	4	0	Colquhoun, Clark, Foster, Robertson
Sept. 27	Dundee	PL	A	0	0	
Oct. 1	Dukla Prague	UEFA	A	0	1	
Oct. 4	Rangers	PL	H	1	1	Berry
Oct. 8	Celtic	PL	A	0	2	
Oct. 11	St Mirren	PL	H	0	0	
Oct. 18	Hamilton	PL	A	3	1	G. Mackay, P, Colquhoun, Foster
Oct. 25	Dundee United	PL	H	2	2	Colquhoun, E. Mackay, P
Oct. 29	Falkirk	PL	A	0	2	—
Nov. 1	Hibernian	PL	H	1	1	G. Mackay, P
Nov. 8	Clydebank	PL	A	3	0	R. McDonald, Colquhoun 2
Nov. 15	Aberdeen	PL	H	2	1	Colquhoun, Robertson
Nov. 19	Motherwell	PL	A	3	2	Berry, R. McDonald 2
Nov. 22	Dundee	PL	H	3	1	Colquhoun, Black, Robertson
Nov. 29	Rangers	PL	A	0	3	
Dec. 3	Celtic	PL	H	1	0	Berry
Dec. 6	St Mirren	PL	A	0	0	
Dec. 13	Hamilton	PL	H	7	0	S. Jardine, Robertson 2, R. McDonald, Colquhoun, Berry, G. Mackay, P
Dec. 20	Dundee United	PL	A	1	3	Robertson
Dec. 27	Falkirk	PL	H	4	0	OG, Robertson 2, Clark
Jan. 3	Clydebank	PL	H	3	0	Clark, G. Mackay, Robertson
Jan. 6	Hibernian	PL	A	2	2	Colquhoun 2
Jan. 21	Aberdeen	PL	A	1	2	Watson
Jan. 24	Dundee	PL	A	1	0	G. Mackay
Jan. 31	Kilmarnock	SCC	H	0	0	
Feb. 4	Kilmarnock	SCC	A	1	1	Foster
Feb. 7	Rangers	PL	H	2	5	Robertson 2
Feb. 9	Kilmarnock	SCC	A	3	1	G. Mackay, Black, Foster
Feb. 14	Celtic	PL	A	1	1	Robertson
Feb. 21	Celtic	SCC	H	1	0	Robertson
Feb. 25	Motherwell	PL	H	1	1	Robertson
Feb. 28	St Mirren	PL	H	1	0	Colquhoun
March 7	Hamilton	PL	A	1	0	Colquhoun
March 14	Motherwell	SCC	H	1	1	Robertson
March 17	Motherwell	SCC	A	1	0	Colquhoun
March 21	Falkirk	PL	A	0	0	
March 28	Clydebank	PL	A	1	1	Colquhoun
April 4	Hibernian	PL	H	2	1	R. McDonald, Clark
April 11	St Mirren	SCC	Hamp	1	2	G. Mackay
April 15	Motherwell	PL	A	1	0	Clark
April 18	Aberdeen	PL	H	1	1	Foster
April 25	Rangers	PL	A	0	3	
May 2	Dundee	PL	H	1	3	Cowie
May 9	Celtic	PL	H	1	0	Robertson, P
May 11	Dundee United	PL	H	1	1	Robertson, P
May 12	Watford	F	A	3	4	Clark, G. Mackay, Robertson, P

FIXTURES, RESULTS, SCORERS 1987/88

Date	Opponents	Comp	Venue	F	A	Scorers
July 19	Hamburg	F	A	1	2	Watson
July 21	Pruessen Munster	F	A	2	0	Mackay, Watson

Date	Opponent	Comp	Venue	F	A	Scorers
July 24	Bad Kreuznach	F	A	3	1	Watson, Moore, Clark
July 25	Birkenfeld	F	A	1	1	Mackay
July 27	Remscheid	F	A	1	2	Robertson
Aug. 1	Berwick Rangers	F	A	2	1	Robertson, McPherson
Aug. 3	Newcastle United	F	H	0	1	
Aug. 8	Falkirk	PL	A	4	2	Robertson 2, Clark, Colquhoun
Aug. 12	Celtic	PL	A	0	1	
Aug. 15	St Mirren	PL	A	1	1	Robertson, P
Aug. 19	Kilmarnock	SC	H	6	1	Clark 2, Foster, Mackay, Berry McPherson
Aug. 22	Dundee United	PL	H	4	1	Clark 2, Robertson, I. Jardine
Aug. 25	Clyde	SC	H	2	0	Robertson 2, 1P
Aug. 29	Hibernian	PL	H	1	0	Robertson
Sept. 2	Rangers	SKC	A	1	4	Robertson
Sept. 5	Morton	PL	A	2	1	Colquhoun, Robertson
Sept. 12	Motherwell	PL	H	1	0	Moore
Sept. 19	Dundee	PL	A	3	1	Colquhoun 2, Robertson, P
Sept. 26	Dunfermline	PL	A	1	0	Colquhoun
Sept. 29	Inverness Caley	F	A	4	3	Burns, Clark, Robertson, Colquoun
Oct. 3	Rangers	PL	H	0	0	
Oct. 7	Aberdeen	PL	H	2	1	Robertson, McPherson
Oct. 10	Falkirk	PL	A	5	1	Foster, Colquhoun 2, I. Jardine, Robertson
Oct. 17	Hibernian	PL	A	1	2	Robertson
Oct. 18	Everton	F	H	1	1	Moore
Oct. 24	Morton	PL	H	3	0	Black 2, Mackay
Oct. 27	Motherwell	PL	A	3	0	Robertson, P, Foster, OG
Oct. 31	Dundee	PL	H	4	2	Robertson 2, Colquhoun, Black
Nov. 7	Celtic	PL	H	1	1	Colquhoun
Nov. 14	Aberdeen	PL	A	0	0	
Nov. 18	Dundee United	PL	A	3	0	Foster, Robertson 2
Nov. 21	St Mirren	PL	H	0	0	
Nov. 24	Dunfermline	PL	H	3	2	McPherson, Clark, Robertson
Nov. 28	Rangers	PL	A	2	3	Galloway, Robertson
Dec. 5	Falkirk	PL	H	1	0	Robertson, P
Dec. 12	Celtic	PL	A	2	2	Robertson, Galloway
Dec. 16	Motherwell	PL	H	1	1	Mackay
Dec. 19	Dundee	PL	A	0	0	
Dec. 26	Morton	PL	A	0	0	
Jan. 2	Hibernian	PL	H	0	0	
Jan. 9	Dunfermline	PL	A	4	0	Galloway, Robertson 2, Colquhoun
Jan. 16	Rangers	PL	H	1	1	Clark
Jan. 30	Falkirk	SC	A	3	1	Robertson 2, Foster
Feb. 3	Dundee United	PL	H	1	1	Mackay
Feb. 6	St Mirren	PL	A	6	0	Colquhoun 3, Robertson 2, Foster
Feb. 13	Aberdeen	PL	H	2	2	Robertson, P, Clark
Feb. 20	Morton	SC	H	2	0	Clark, Mackay
Feb. 27	Falkirk	PL	A	0	2	
March 8	Motherwell	PL	A	2	0	Robertson, Colquhoun
March 12	Dunfermline	SC	H	3	0	Colquhoun, Foster, Mackay
March 19	Hibernian	PL	A	0	0	
March 26	Morton	PL	H	2	0	Galloway 2
March 30	Dundee	PL	H	2	0	Colquhoun, Black
April 2	Rangers	PL	A	2	1	Robertson, P, McPherson
April 9	Celtic	SC	Hamp	1	2	Whittaker
April 13	Dunfermline	PL	H	2	1	Mackay, McPherson
April 16	Celtic	PL	H	2	1	Mackay, Galloway
April 23	Aberdeen	PL	A	0	0	
April 24	Falkirk Select	F	A	2	4	A. McDonald, Black, P
April 30	St Mirren	PL	H	0	1	
May 7	Dundee United	PL	A	0	0	
May 8	Hibernian	ESS	A	5	1	Berry 2, Moore 2, Docherty

FIXTURES, RESULTS, SCORERS 1988/89

Date	Opponents	Comp	Venue	F	A	Scorers
July 13	T.S.V. Battenburg	F	A	3	3	Crabbe, Galloway, Mackay, P
July 15	Rot-Weiss Essen	F	A	1	1	Galloway
July 16	Fort Dusseldorf	F	A	0	1	
July 20	Reimshied	F	A	2	0	I. Jardine, Clark
July 23	A.S.C. Schoeppingen	F	A	2	2	Black, Gavin
July 24	Zielpich	F	A	4	2	Galloway, Clark 2, Colquhoun
July 30	Forres Mechanics	F	A	5	1	Ferguson, Foster, Galloway 2, Mackay
Aug. 1	Lossiemouth	F	A	4	0	OG, Colquhoun, Ferguson, Foster
Aug. 6	Airdrieonians	F	A	5	0	Galloway, Clark, Colquhoun, Ferguson, I. Jardine
Aug. 9	Cruzeiro	F	H	2	1	Ferguson, Black, P
Aug. 13	Celtic	PL	A	0	1	
Aug. 17	St Johnstone	SKC	H	5	0	Mackay, Ferguson 3, I. Jardine
Aug. 20	Hamilton	PL	H	3	2	Colquhoun, Clark, Ferguson
Aug. 23	Meadowbank	SKC	A	2	0	Murray, Black
Aug. 27	Hibernian	PL	A	0	0	
Aug. 31	Dunfermline	SKC	A	4	1	Colquhoun, Mackay, Ferguson 2
Sept. 3	St Mirren	PL	H	1	2	Foster, P
Sept. 7	St Patrick's	UEFA	A	2	0	Galloway, Foster (P)
Sept. 12	Nottingham Forest	F	H	0	3	
Sept. 17	Rangers	PL	H	1	2	OG
Sept. 21	Rangers	SCC	Hamp	0	3	
Sept. 24	Aberdeen	PL	A	0	1	
Sept. 28	Dundee	PL	H	1	1	Ferguson
Oct. 1	Dundee United	PL	A	0	0	
Oct. 5	St Patrick's	UEFA	H	2	0	Galloway, Black
Oct. 8	Motherwell	PL	H	2	2	Moore 2,
Oct. 11	Hamilton	PL	A	4	0	Ferguson 2, Black, Colquhoun
Oct. 22	Celtic	PL	H	0	2	
Oct. 26	F.K. Austria Vienna	UEFA	H	0	0	
Oct. 29	Aberdeen	PL	H	1	1	I. Jardine
Nov. 2	Rangers	PL	A	0	3	
Nov. 5	St Mirren	PL	H	1	1	OG
Nov. 9	F.K. Austria Vienna	UEFA	A	1	0	Galloway
Nov. 12	Hibernian	PL	H	1	2	McPherson
Nov. 19	Dundee United	PL	A	0	0	
Nov. 23	Velez Mostar	UEFA	H	3	0	Bannon, Galloway, Colquhoun
Nov. 26	Motherwell	PL	A	0	2	
Dec. 3	Dundee	PL	A	1	1	Colquhoun
Dec. 7	Velez Mostar	UEFA	A	1	2	Galloway
Dec. 10	Rangers	PL	H	2	0	Ferguson, Galloway
Dec. 17	Hamilton	PL	H	2	0	McPherson, McLaren
Dec. 18	Dunfermline	F	A	5	3	Ferguson 2, Galloway 2, Foster
Dec. 31	Celtic	PL	A	2	4	Robertson 2, 1P
Jan. 4	Hibernian	PL	A	0	1	
Jan. 7	St Mirren	PL	H	2	0	Colquhoun, McKinlay
Jan. 14	Motherwell	PL	H	0	0	
Jan. 21	Dundee United	PL	A	0	0	
Jan. 28	Ayr United	SCC	H	4	1	McPherson, Galloway, Colquhoun, OG
Feb. 11	Dundee	PL	H	3	1	Bannon, Colquhoun, Mackay
Feb. 18	Partick Th.	SCC	H	2	0	Bannon, Colquhoun
Feb. 25	Aberdeen	PL	A	0	3	
Feb. 28	Bayern Munich	UEFA	H	1	0	Ferguson
March 11	Celtic	PL	H	0	1	
March 14	Bayern Munich	UEFA	A	0	2	
March 18	Celtic	SCC	A	1	2	Bannon
March 25	Hamilton	PL	A	2	0	McPherson, Mackay
April 1	Hibernian	PL	H	2	1	Bannon, Robertson
April 8	St Mirren	PL	A	1	1	Robertson

Date						
April 15	Dundee	PL	A	1	2	McPherson
April 22	Aberdeen	PL	H	1	0	Galloway
April 29	Rangers	PL	A	0	4	
May 6	Dundee United	PL	H	0	0	
May 13	Motherwell	PL	A	1	1	Berry

FIXTURES, RESULTS, SCORERS 1989/90

Date	Opponents	Comp	Venue	F	A	Scorers
July 29	Nairn County	F	A	5	1	McPherson, Colquhoun, Ferguson, Crabbe 2
July 31	Inverness Caley	F	A	3	2	Mackay, Ferguson, Kirkwood
Aug. 2	Peterhead	F	A	4	0	Ferguson 2, Musemic, Berry
Aug. 5	Sunderland	F	H	1	0	Musemic
Aug. 8	Dynamo Tbilisi	F	H	0	2	
Aug. 12	Celtic	PL	H	1	3	McPherson
Aug. 16	Montrose	SKC	H	3	0	Crabbe 2, Musemic
Aug. 19	St Mirren	PL	A	2	1	Musemic
Aug. 23	Falkirk	SKC	A	4	1	Kidd, Kirkwood, Crabbe, Bannon
Aug. 26	Hibernian	PL	H	1	0	Musemic
Aug. 30	Celtic	SKC	A	2	2	Crabbe, Robertson
Sept. 9	Dundee	PL	A	2	2	McPherson, Crabbe, P
Sept. 16	Motherwell	PL	A	3	1	Crabbe 2, Robertson
Sept. 23	Dundee United	PL	H	1	1	McPherson
Sept. 26	Manchester United	F	H	2	4	Crabbe, Bannon, P
Sept. 30	Rangers	PL	A	0	1	
Oct. 4	Dunfermline	PL	H	1	2	Musemic
Oct. 14	Aberdeen	PL	A	3	1	McKinlay, Crabbe 2
Oct. 21	Celtic	PL	A	1	2	Crabbe
Oct. 28	St Mirren	PL	H	4	0	Robertson 2, Crabbe, Colquhoun
Nov. 4	Hibernian	PL	A	1	1	Bannon
Nov. 11	Dundee	PL	H	6	3	Colquhoun 3, Foster, Robertson, Crabbe
Nov. 18	Motherwell	PL	H	3	0	Sandison, Colquhoun, Crabbe
Nov. 25	Dundee United	PL	A	1	2	Crabbe, P
Dec. 2	Rangers	PL	H	1	2	Bannon
Dec. 9	Dunfermline	PL	A	2	0	Robertson 2
Dec. 20	Aberdeen	PL	H	1	1	Robertson
Dec. 26	Celtic	PL	H	0	0	
Dec. 30	St Mirren	PL	A	0	2	
Jan. 1	Hibernian	PL	H	2	0	Robertson 2, 1P
Jan. 6	Dundee	PL	A	1	0	Colquhoun
Jan. 13	Motherwell	PL	A	3	0	Robertson 2, 1P, Colquhoun
Jan. 20	Falkirk	SC	H	2	0	Robertson 2
Jan. 27	Dundee United	PL	H	3	2	Kidd, Robertson, P Crabbe
Feb. 3	Aberdeen	PL	A	2	2	Sandison, Ferguson
Feb. 10	Dunfermline	PL	H	0	2	
Feb. 17	Rangers	PL	A	0	0	
Feb. 24	Motherwell	SC	H	4	0	Robertson 2, Crabbe, Colquhoun
March 3	Motherwell	PL	H	2	0	Robertson, Crabbe
March 10	Celtic	PL	A	1	1	Robertson
March 17	Aberdeen	SC	A	1	4	Colquhoun
March 24	St Mirren	PL	H	0	0	
March 31	Hibernian	PL	A	2	1	Robertson 2
April 4	Dundee	PL	H	0	0	
April 14	Dunfermline	PL	A	1	0	McPherson
April 21	Aberdeen	PL	H	1	0	Mackay
April 28	Dundee United	PL	A	1	1	McLaren
May 3	Hibernian	ESS	A	0	0	
May 5	Rangers	PL	H	1	1	Robertson